Comments made about the book

"A significant book because of the insight it brings to the reader of the complexity of relationships, and trauma for the cared for and the carer with fostering children. This book entertains, educates and arouses all sorts of emotions for the reader. It is also an inspirational book as it sends out messages of hope that there are some people who care a lot about others and have the patience and courage to support and offer a decent framework for those who need it."

"Written with clarity and without drama, it's an easy read, but so disturbing. Few people appreciate how mistreatment can result in the most inexplicable behaviour in even very young children. It's important that parents and anyone involved in the caring professions or even thinking about it, should be aware, and this honest and frank book will certainly help achieve that..."

"Touching and effective. Written well, and at a pace that reads very well; I hope this does well."

"Not only is the detail in this book an elemental draw, the writing style has much to commend it simply on style and structured pace alone."

"It is the eye for detail that marks this out as a crafted piece as well as an interesting non-fiction story."

"This is a touching, gritty true story. Thought provoking. Vivid scenes. Evocative narrative. Confident writing."

"This is a story that has been so well told. When I say story I mean it in the non-fiction sense. Honest, open, real, heartrending."

"Tormented is presented in business-like but graphic detail and there is no doubt as to the validity of the story contained therein. Painful experiences are vividly described and the difficulties encountered in attempting to analyse the behaviour and thought processes of foster children, influenced as they are by previous 'care and attention', are identified. This work is competent and knowledgeable and is virtually an informal treatise."

Tormented

Lizzie Scott has asserted her right to be identified as the author of this Work in accordance with the Copyright, Designs and Patents Act 1988

All rights reserved.

No part of this publication may be reproduced, stored in a retrieval system, or transmitted, in any form or by any means, electronic, mechanical, photocopying, recording or otherwise, without the prior permission in writing of the copyright owner, nor be otherwise circulated in any form of binding or cover other than that in which it is published and without a similar condition including this condition being imposed on the subsequent purchaser.

This, my first book is dedicated to

Howard, David, Edward, James and Claire.

You are the air that I breathe

Thank you all for being the very special people that you are

All names have been changed to protect the identities of the innocent.

May you always have an angel by your side,
Watching out for you in all the things you do,
Reminding you to keep believing in brighter days,
Finding ways for your wishes and dreams
To take you to beautiful places,
Giving you hope that is as certain as the sun,
And giving you the strength of serenity as your
guide.

May you always have an angel by your side,
Someone there to catch you if you fall,
Encouraging your dreams, inspiring your happiness,
Holding your hand and helping you through it all.

In all of our days, our lives are always changing;
Tears come along as well as smiles.
Along the roads you travel, may the miles
Be a thousand times more lovely than lonely.
May they give you the kind of Christmas gifts that
never ever end;
Someone wonderful to love and a dear friend
In whom you can confide.
May you have rainbows after every storm
And hope to keep you warm.

May you always have love,
Comfort and courage...
And may you always have an
Angel by your side!

Author Unknown

Chapter 1

I'd had the phone call on Tuesday, enquiring when the boys we were fostering were leaving. Having told the social worker they were due to return to their family on the following Monday, I'd been asked to consider looking after two little girls.

I told the social worker that, in theory, we would have them. Now I would need to discuss the placement with my husband, and weigh up the implications on our own children, as our six year old daughter Claire was used to being the only 'little lady' in our home. Though our children always welcomed each new 'brother' or 'sister' with open arms, foster parents have to think about the possibility of disrupted nights and the open aggression that some children bring with them.

Jealousies can also arouse from either our children or our fostered children and of course, the change in routine that happens with each new placement. Consideration has also to be given to such things as fitting in our children's after school activities and supporting children who have contact in or away from our home.

We also had to speak with our eldest son David, who was settled at university but still came home for the odd weekend when he wasn't busy studying, or carrying out one of the many pursuits he had taken up over the past year.

There was also the added concern that due to Jenny's age she would attend the same school as Claire. This had caused a small issue with a previous placement, though Claire and Vikki, being the same age had been in the same class which had meant Claire had no time away from her. At least with the age difference Claire would get lesson time away from Jenny.

Julia, the social worker explained that the children had been bought to England from Wales, where they had been living with their grandparents, but couldn't return there, now having given me as much information as she could, we ended the phone call.

Monday morning arrived quickly, our youngest sons Edward and James as well as Claire had been taken to school and I was busy packing the last few bits of clothes and toys ready for the social worker to take the boys home to their parents.

It had been lovely having them in our home, but it was always much nicer to have a happy ending to a placement; however that was reached, return or adoption was better than long term care.

Once the boys had left I got on with changing the beds and sorting out wardrobe space for the girls.

I also climbed into the loft to sort out a special 'cuddle' to leave on the girls' beds.

I made sure to always keep a large supply of soft cuddly toys up there as experience had taught us the children we cared for seldom arrived with anything to comfort them once they had gone to bed and we knew, irrespective of the children's age, a soft toy was usually hugged tightly if only while the children were settling in to their new home and the older children, only if they thought we couldn't see them.

Once that was done I set about tidying up the playroom, making sure I left out some toys for the girls.

Howard and I had discussed the issues that Julia had told me about.

On the surface there seemed little to concern us.

Having been asked if we would facilitate contact at our home, we felt fairly confident that this was going to be an 'okay' family, one which we would form a relationship with and at some time in the future, start working towards the girls returning home to either their mother or extended family members.

Once we had decided this was a placement we could work with, we had asked the children if they would like two little girls to stay.

Obviously, being bound by the constraints of confidentiality and our children's ages we didn't tell them about any of the issues, though pointed out that it would mean Claire would be sharing her bedroom with two little girls and it was more likely that they would want to play with her toys and spend time with her.

We always explained to our children that sharing a room meant that they may have disturbed nights, the child may mess their things up or break their toys. They may also steal from them and many had night terrors and wet the bed. Basic information, but important as the last thing we wanted was for any child to have more moves than necessary within the care system, as each move was, to the children we cared for, a rejection.

Once our family had committed to a placement, we stayed committed.

Our children knew that and as young as they were, without realising it, supported Howard and I in the work we chose to do.

Julia arrived with the girls just after 2pm. Even though it was the first time we had met, we had spoken so often on the telephone during the past week about the girls; I felt I knew her well already.

Julia was a bit taller than me, quite slim and blond. She had a relaxed air about her and a ready smile that reached her eyes. The best thing was she made me feel like she was talking to an equal, something so many social workers didn't quite manage.

Since we had started fostering, so many social workers we'd worked with had spoken to us as though we were one up from the client whose child we were caring for. This was a common complaint from many of the foster carers we had met at the monthly support group I attended at the time.

The girls had been in care for just over a week, staying in what is termed as an 'emergency placement'.

As a rule I don't like having children from emergency placements. This is my own prejudice I know, but it's because it means another move for the children, another 'felt' rejection.

Another down side to taking emergency placements meant that, if the child had been placed for a few weeks, their previous carer had probably been given the clothing allowance, though many didn't send the items purchased for the children with them when they moved on, which could mean quite a considerable financial outlay for my husband as we felt it was important that the children feel part of our family, not only by being included in whatever we were doing, but by looking as though they belonged as well.

Not that our children were ever togged out in designer gear, but they always had nice clothes and looked presentable.

Irrespective of your own personality, society does notice clothes and we had found that a child that dresses similar to their peers is more likely to be accepted by them, especially if joining a classroom where friendships have already been formed.

Commitment is paramount in making a child feel valued and I feel very strongly that should start from day one.

Howard and I also provided emergency cover for the department, which happens when a child suddenly needs to be found somewhere safe to stay without prior planning or warning, but, in general, these children then stayed until their future was sorted out.

The downside to providing emergency placements is that the children come home, or wake in the morning, to an enlarged family with no warning and absolutely no knowledge about age, sex or minor problems they may have to cope with.

Fortunately most of our placements were planned and the emergency ones worked out well, thanks to us knowing our children's expectations of their parents and, in the case of daytime emergencies, me knowing how relaxed and accepting Howard was of any decision I made regarding sharing our life and home.

Jenny, aged 5, and Chloe, aged 3 came running up the drive showing no outward concerns about moving into our home.

Even though we had not been foster parents for many years, we were concerned this was a clear indication of an 'attachment disorder'; one more issue we would have to work with as we helped these children come to terms with their past and move on to a better future.

Attachment is a very complex area and can manifest in many different ways. Some children can't even refer to their siblings by their names, preferring to simply say "My brother or my sister", some will sit on the sidelines of life, watching but not participating in activities that they may well enjoy, for fear of a positive reaction that they will not understand or be able to cope with.

Many will deliberately sabotage all attempts to form good relationships because they 'know' they are not worth anything to anyone, and you are just lying to them anyway, just getting ready to dump them like everyone else has. It's just easier if they never get close to you, then you can't hurt them can you.

A child's ability to relate to others and build relationships can depend on the quality of their early childhood relationships and the trauma they may have experienced.

Though not all apparent irrational behaviours and reactions can be attributed to attachment disorder, it's a good area to look at. It's a good base to begin forming a bond with the child and help them experience the joy of positive attention and praise for good behaviour, rather than avoiding it, though this does need patience as it can take a long time.

As I watched the children coming towards me my initial thoughts, apart from concern at their friendliness, was how pretty they were.

Both had lovely dark hair and pretty blue eyes. They appeared to be dressed nicely and were clean, another plus as most of the children we cared for needed a nice warm bath and change of clothes almost on arrival, not that you could do that as it could be seen as a form of rejection in their eyes, of all that is familiar to them.

No, usually when a child arrived we let them play, explore our home and settle in before having a meal, bath and bedtime story.

Day two was always the start of getting to know them and settling into a routine which would allow for any changes that would evolve slowly as our relationship and hopefully, the child's trust in us grew.

Once the children and Julia were in our home I showed the children into the playroom, while Julia and I sat in the lounge which was the adjoining room, discussing the expectations the department had of us, and ours of them.

Neither Julia nor I were aware as we sat chatting just how harrowing this placement was to become over the following months.

Chapter 2

Julia left after about an hour and the children, on hearing Julia saying she would say goodbye to them, ran out of the playroom to wave her off before running back to play with the toys.

Once I had shut the front door I followed them into the playroom to find they had totally trashed it; pulling all the toys out of cupboards, dumping the games out of the boxes and ripping books off the bookcase. Every item that was on or in the desk where the children sat to do their homework, or art work was also over the floor; pens, paper, rubbers and paperclips. Thank goodness the computer was still where it should have been.

I felt quite shocked at the devastation they had wreaked in such a short time. And they had been so quiet that Julia and I thought they were simply playing nicely. In all honesty I had never seen the playroom in such a mess and knew my children would be terribly upset to see all their 'treasures' so badly treated.

My whole family were avid readers and to see the children's books just thrown around and torn or scribbled in was quite upsetting. Clearly these two lovely looking little girls were going to need very close supervision and clear boundaries set and set quickly.

As I tidied the room and got ready to take the girls to school to meet our children, Jenny played with the Cindy dolls and the doll's house.

Suddenly she held up a Cindy doll, said her baby had been sick on the bed and that a man had killed her. When she took her to the doctor she wasn't dead, but a monster was going to get her.

Jenny also said that her granddad had told her she would never go to him again and both of her grandparents were crying because of this.

As time was moving on and we had to get to the school I didn't have time to dwell on this conversation, though as monsters were to feature a lot in Jenny's vocabulary for the duration of this placement I wish I had.

It is most unfortunate that so many children will start to disclose information that is important, at a time when you can't sit and progress the conversation or game they are enacting.

This is quite a clever ploy these children learn.

They 'test' the water to see if they can trust you, revisiting their issues when they feel more secure, safe and settled.

With everything that was going on over the coming days and weeks it would be a little while before I could revisit this time.

Reflective thought is a wonderful thing though and although the opportunity to talk with the girls about their first day with us didn't present itself for a while I thought about what had been said and how they had played with the toys over the following weeks.

There are usually signs in how the children react to different situations and conversations that can indicate some of the areas you, as a foster carer, will need to work.

I knew that the very least we had to do was teach these children the three 'R's...Respect for self, respect for other's and responsibility for their own actions.

I also checked through what the children had bought with them...a carrier bag of socks, all different sizes and not one matching pair; on trouser suit which though nice was far to big for either of them and a few toys.

We would have to do some clothes shopping on the way to or from the school to get some nightwear and a change of clothes for the next day at least.

Luckily I'm an absolute shopaholic for childrens clothes so this was something I knew I'd enjoy and hoped Jenny and Chloe would.

We don't have a lot of shops in the area we live, so I have a good relationship with the few that sell childrens clothes and know the staff well.

As usual when I go shopping I was greeted as I entered the first shop and the staff chatted with the girls as I piled up the items we were purchasing on the counter.

I managed to get everything I needed in the one shop, remembering to get a little something for our sons Edward who was aged ten, James who was aged eight and for our daughter Claire as well so they wouldn't feel left out of the 'treat', though I think for most of the children that shared our home, the 'treat' for them was normality for us...a warm bed, regular meals, clean clothes, baths and someone that would play with them and listen to them around all the time.

Fortunately, I also had a good relationship with our local primary schools. I had managed to secure Jenny a place, knowing that she would get full support from the headmistress and staff, as they had done with all our foster children over the past four years.

It was simply a case of popping in to introduce Jenny to the school and her teacher. It was agreed that she would start the following Monday, giving her a week to settle into her new home and surroundings.

I had also approached one of the local playschools and Chloe was to start the on the same day.

We had a nice, though noisy evening with five children in the house.

The three girls seemed able to make more noise than the five boys we had only yesterday!

When it was time for bed Howard, my husband, read the children a story and we tucked them in.

They were sharing our daughter's bedroom and the three girls settled quickly to sleep.

However, they didn't sleep for long.

By 11.20pm they had been in and out of their beds so many times to get different toys to play with, use the bathroom, ask for a drink, report monsters under the beds and just to ask if it was morning yet that I was knackered, though I figured if this kept up it was cheaper than going to the gym!

And Claire, being a heavy sleeper, slept through it all.

Howard and I finally got to bed just after midnight.

It was 2am when I woke.

I don't know what woke me as the house was quiet.

I checked the children's bedrooms, covering Claire as she had wriggled out of bed.

I quickly checked the bunk beds and Jenny and Chloe appeared to be tucked in as we had left them.

I then checked the boys who were still tucked up and sleeping peacefully in their rooms.

As I got back into my bed I still felt uneasy so decided to check the children again.

This time I gently eased the covers down a little on the bottom bunk.

Chloe wasn't there.

I did the same with the top bunk and felt alarm rising as both beds were empty.

I quietly left the room so as not to disturb Claire and ran down the stairs.

Bugger, bugger, bugger.

What if the girls have opened the door and run away?

My heart was racing as I quietly ran downstairs.

The downside to having double glazed doors is that they don't facilitate bolts.

To lock the house safely you need to use a key and I didn't like the idea of being locked in a house at night and not having the key in the door.

This goes back to when I was a child and our home had caught fire early one morning.

Though no-one in my family was hurt and the fire was quickly contained, the fear of not being able to get out in an emergency has stayed.

Therefore, we simply pushed the handle up which set the deadbolts, but didn't actually lock it.

That meant all the children had to do was pull the handle down to open it.

I heaved a sigh of relief when I saw the front door was shut and I went through the lounge into the playroom.

I wished I'd had my camera with me because there, sitting on top of every toy, every game, every book, pencil, crayon, just everything that was in the room, were Jenny and Chloe, oblivious to everything, colouring in a picture.

My relief that they hadn't opened the front door and gone outside was so great that I couldn't even be angry with them, even though it meant another major clean up job in the morning and some more complaints from our own children.

When I asked them to go back to bed they very quietly did as I asked and settled to sleep...while I stayed awake listening, for hours.

We were to find during the following days that Jenny had a very stubborn streak and we had to be very firm with boundaries for her. She had to learn that no meant no, not maybe in a little while. We had quite a few occasions when it seemed Jenny and I were having a battle of wills and though sometimes I would want to back down just so we could have a little normality back, I knew that the first time I did, I would lose more than one little battle and Jenny would have more power than she would know how to handle.

No, Jenny had to learn that adults do the parenting. Adults make the decisions, however nice or nasty they may seem, while children play and have fun.

She would play happily on her own or with the other children, but if I asked her to do anything that she didn't want to she would play deaf, or worse than that, she would stare through you as though you were not on the same planet, let alone the same room. I had to quickly find strategies to manage this behaviour without letting her know what I was doing. Sometimes I chose to pretend I hadn't noticed and would re-phrase a request after a couple of minutes had passed. This seemed to work well, though not always, and then we would have the battle of wills and sanctions used such as no television for the evening. In many ways this was punishing me, as if Jenny had been particularly stressful it meant I had to keep her with me, while the other children watched their programme in peace or played with their toys and sometimes, well, to be honest, most times when her behaviour was that naughty, I didn't want her with me. I needed time out as well, but the lesson had to be learnt and I was definitely no lazy parent who would 'forget' to carry out sanctions for a peaceful life.

She was also over friendly with everyone; whether they were visitors to our home or strangers we passed in the street.

Everyone was Jenny's friend as far as she was concerned.

Jenny was also quite bossy towards her little sister, ordering her around and telling her off if she thought she'd been naughty.

Chloe on the other hand appeared to be a most loving little girl, quite tearful and clingy and needing reassurance that all was okay in her world.

Chloe had the largest eyes ever and the most endearing smile to go with them. If you asked her to do something she would usually run to please you. She would happily play with anyone that would give her the time and even if I was doing housework would give me a running commentary on what was going on in her games.

Chloe loved to be clean and have nice clothes on. Jenny didn't seem to notice what she was wearing. Chloe would let you play with her hair, jenny just wanted it brushed and to be away and doing whatever she wanted to do as quickly as possible.

Chloe would happily share the toys with the other children.

That is until my nephew and niece arrived one day to play.

She grabbed my niece who was only 15 months old and shook her so violently I though her head would fall off!

Chloe didn't like to share with 'outsiders'.

Chapter 3

The first week of having Jenny and Chloe live with us was in all honesty, totally exhausting.

Jenny wet the bed most nights, went through several pairs of knickers during the day and was generally uncooperative or downright rude to me, though was a little darling when Howard was home. It hadn't taken long for her to realise what time Howard arrived home from work and, if she was going to test my patience she would do so until five minutes before he walked through the door, when she would 'turn off' negative behaviours and act like a little angel so he would wonder at what had vexed me so.

Jenny also talked of monsters all the time, saying her dad was one (though we were not aware she knew who her dad was). No matter what she was playing there seemed to be a monster of some sort involved.

One day she suddenly piped up that her granddad was nice because he gave her biscuits in the dark, which immediately set off alarm bells in my head.

I had to be careful not to let her notice this.

Unfortunately she shut up as soon as she said this, leaving me no opening to get her talking again as she ran off to play with Claire.

Another snippet of information we would have to revisit at a later date.

Chloe remained quite clingy, not wanting to be alone with Jenny, though not wanting her out of her sights either.

Chloe would also have bad dreams and wake up crying, saying she thought someone had hurt her.

When I asked if she knew who it was she said she did, though no amount of gentle coaxing would get her to open up.

On the fourth day of placement Jenny had just wet herself for the second time.

While I helped her change out of her wet knickers she wet herself again; all over me.

As I got another pair of dry knickers I asked why she'd wet again and she told me she did the same to her granddad and he hurt her.

I asked where he hurt her and she pointed to her arms, back, legs and bottom.

I asked her what room she was in when her granddad hurt her and she told me the bedroom.

She explained she was sick on him because he was hurting her and pulling her hair.

She said she hid her head under the blanket but tried to be nice to him because he gave her sweets.

How I managed to chat away normally whilst covered in pee surprised me as I don't consider myself the most patient of people, but had come to realise that normality for the average child is nowhere near normality to the child in care.

I also felt sick to the core as I realised these two little girls had possibly been sexually abused by their grandfather.

I could feel the anger rising inside of me.

I could feel the utter helplessness of their situation.

I wanted to hit out physically at an adult, a trusted adult that could hurt an innocent child so badly.

But most of all I just wanted to cry for them and what they had been through.

To cry for me and the secrets they would give to me at some time in order for them to move forward.

I wanted to cry for my pain and my fear at what had happened in their little lives.

When we were on our own I spoke to Howard about Jenny's behaviour and the things she had said.

He knew my anger and frustration as he felt them too.

As a man he could not understand how anyone could find children 'exciting' in a sexual way.

Our fear at that time was that Jenny would tell our children some of her 'secrets'.

We had learned that children sometimes disclose to their peers.

This was not something we wanted to happen in our family, though we couldn't say to Jenny and Chloe "Don't talk to Edward, James and Claire about when you lived with your grandparents" as that may be seen as a weapon to use against us if we used the 'no' word to them, well, to Jenny as Chloe did not appear to be into 'power' games.

Our children knew though that if they were given a secret by a child living with us, no matter how silly, rude or naughty it sounded, they had to tell us.

The only secrets in our home, was what we had bought as Birthday or Christmas presents.

As a treat for all the children we decided to take them to London on Saturday, reasoning that we may get a good night's sleep if we tired Jenny and Chloe out.

It also meant that David, home for the weekend, could enjoy a family day out, something we didn't get enough of with him living so far away.

We had a great day out and, after spending about eight hours traipsing round the sights; going up St Pauls Cathedral and having a snack on a boat we finally arrived home with five exhausted children and had our first complete night's sleep since the girls arrived.

On Sunday we went to church. We went most Sundays, meeting Howard's parents there and they usually came home after the service for an hour or two.

Jenny and Chloe went into junior church with our children part way through the service, returning at the end of the service to show the adult congregation any artwork they had done.

Jenny and Chloe seemed to enjoy themselves and were eager to return the following Sunday, which was great as it meant we could keep this bit of important routine normality.

And so finally the first week was over.

Jenny and Chloe appeared to have settled quite well into our family and were getting used to the boundaries that our children had.

On the whole they were very good children, they just had some big problems which, until we understood them, we would have to live with the behaviour they presented.

Chapter 4

It didn't take long for Jenny to settle in to school life. She went to the same school as Claire, though was in the year below. Jenny liked her teacher and thankfully, her teacher liked her.

On the Tuesday I was called into the school to discuss a small problem that had arisen.

Oh dear...day two and problems already. This didn't bode well.

Jenny had sat on her teacher's lap and soiled herself......twice.

The school were very supportive but needed to know if I knew why she would do this.

I could offer no explanation as we hadn't had the soiling at home, though I made them aware that she often wet herself. I couldn't tell them what my fears were about their past, only ask that they be vigilant of Jennies behaviours and let me know if she displayed any that caused them concern.

For the duration of the school term Jenny would wet and soil herself on an almost daily basis.

The support I received from the school was just amazing though because they didn't expel her; the teacher simply took a fresh change of clothes with her each day so if she should get caught out when Jenny climbed on her lap for a cuddle, she could change her clothes as well as Jenny getting changed.

I don't know if Jenny's teacher was aware of how important this tactic was.

She could so easily have just refused to allow Jenny to sit on her lap but that would possibly have been seen by Jenny as yet another rejection and, at the time, I honestly don't think even Jenny understood why she behaved as she did.

As well as Jenny settling into school Chloe settled well into playschool, enjoying the new toys and having other children her age to play with.

Chloe started to respond well to simple requests, like putting toys away at mealtimes and bedtimes, but Jenny remained oblivious to most request made of her, only reacting when offered something to eat or drink.

One day at school Jenny wet herself, soaking her dress as well as her panties. When she was being helped into dry clothes she ran off down the corridor ignoring the teachers request to return and behave.

As Jenny's behaviour could be so erratic it was lovely to watch as Chloe seemed to blossom, she had a ready smile for everyone who knew her, though unlike Jenny, she was wary of people she didn't know.

Chloe, like Jenny concerned me in the way she played at times with her 'babies', covering them with a blanket and saying they were dead.

She never elaborated, just stated that they were dead and moved on to another game.

It was toward the end of the second week of placement that I met their mum.

Susan presented as quite a shy person but was openly affectionate towards the children, who appeared pleased to see her.

As had been agreed before the children arrived, contact would be once a month at our home.

Depending on the child's known background social workers will assess whether this is in the children's best interest.

If at all possible it is a more relaxed occasion for children to spend time with their birth family in an environment that is known to them and with people they have some relationship with, rather than at a family centre with a member of staff.

This arrangement not only benefits the children but also frees the family centre to supervise the more difficult or challenging families that the department care for.

The down side to having contact within the foster home is the possible removal of a safe place for the children to live. This isn't a physical removal due to the child having to move to a new foster carer for fear of a snatch or reprisals by birth family, but an emotional one caused because their safe home has become 'violated' by the mere fact that birth family have been there, sat on the furniture, shared a meal and even possibly tucked them up in bed.

In other words, that we had accepted them. We had to be very aware of how we acted around birth family. We had to show respect, regardless of our personal feelings, so the birth family didn't complain about our actions, yet at the same time let the children know that they and their feelings came first before those of their birth family.

Susan was quite attentive towards Jenny and Chloe, encouraging Chloe to eat when she decided she'd play up and playing with them after they had eaten.

After tea she got them ready for bed and settled them in with a bedtime story.

This was a big mistake which I wouldn't understand for many weeks to come, but being a relative rooky in this job I had a lot to learn and boy, this placement was going to be my learning curve.

Within an hour of going to bed Jenny woke up crying uncontrollably, taking a long time to comfort and settle again.

Jenny needed so much reassurance that she was safe and there were no monsters in her bedroom or anywhere in the house.

Chloe was unsettled and cried in her sleep throughout the night.

By the morning I was knackered and in no mood for the tantrum that Chloe threw because she didn't want to walk to school with the older children.

Chloe then had an accident prone day and kept falling over at playschool and to end the day off, they trashed the playroom in five minutes while I was serving up their tea.

Following this contact we had a week of Chloe crying in her sleep and Jenny being quite destructive with the toys and ignoring me more than usual.

Four days after contact Jenny was playing nicely with the baby dolls.

She wrapped the doll up and suddenly started to shout at it to go to sleep.

She then started thumping it and kicking it around the room.

I explained to her that we don't hurt babies or baby dolls, but cuddle them to sleep.

Jenny just laughed and walked away.

I noticed during this period that Jenny rarely actually wet herself, but seemed to have a permanent leak.

It was also during this time that Jenny started to trust me just a little and talk about her family.

She told me that she didn't like her granddad because he was naughty to her, and that he hurt her in his house.

She said there was a machine in granddad's house for clothes, she had been put in it and her hair was all over the place.

Jenny wasn't saying much still, but at least she had started.

I explained gently about good and bad secrets, good and bad touches and told her that she could get rid of bad secrets by talking to me or Howard, her teachers or her social worker, whoever she felt was 'safe', because bad secrets can hurt inside and they are just not nice to carry round.

Of course, this talking also led to some negative behaviours; getting up through the night and running around shouting as she threw things around.

It was pretty amazing that the other children slept through most of it, though on reflection I suppose they had got so used to the noise that it had become 'normal' to them.

It has also become normal for me to change the beds on an almost daily basis as both girls now not only wet the bed but sometimes would get out of bed to pee all over the carpet, which I suppose, being logical, makes sense as it meant they had a dry bed to sleep in.

Unfortunately logic can get lost when you know as you climb into bed that tomorrow will probably be another day of changing beds and challenging behaviour.

A day of trying to appease your own children as they watch quite bewildered at the behaviours they witnessed and their parents at a loss as to what to do next.

A day when your commitment may just waver too much and you hold your hands up in desperation and say 'Enough!'

We just knew though that we couldn't do that.

Not to these children.

Not to any child.

We just had to keep focused on the fact that these children were a product of their early years.

Nothing they did was their fault... well; the reasons at least were not their fault.

And so life progressed.

We got used to wet beds, soggy carpets, (soggy me and soggy teachers), Jenny shouting and running through the house at night with the screaming abdabs and Chloe crying out in her sleep.

Howard and I were knackered but the children did seem to be calming down, albeit for only a few days at a time, but it was progress.

Jenny and Chloe had also started to expose themselves to each other, laughing as they did so and saying how rude they were.

Jenny was also speaking more about her life with her granddad and one day told me that he 'licked' her.

I thought I'd misheard her at first and asked if she meant liked, but she was sure it was licked so I asked her where.

Jenny pointed to her arms, nose, mouth and tummy.

Then said her granddad took her knickers off and licked her but she didn't like it when he did that.

I gave Jenny loads of reassurance that she was a very good girl for telling me what her granddad did, and reassured her that she was safe in our home and nothing like that would happen here.

The sick feeling that I'd felt early on in this placement returned.

The anger and helplessness I'd known when Jenny first spoke of her past.

I felt useless because I couldn't take any of these experiences away and pretty hopeless because I had little experience of caring for children that had been so damaged by people they should have been able to trust to care for them properly and to protect them.

I also felt the frustration of knowing these children would live with this for the rest of their lives.

Oh yes, I know all the theory about 'victims and survivors'.

I also knew that even survivors of abuse experience 'flashbacks'.

That even with counselling, one day a word or action would bring everything flooding back and the nightmare would be lived through again.

I reported all the things Jenny told me to their social worker, Julia, who was pro active in getting whatever support she could for the girls.

Nowadays there are therapists almost on hand and therapeutic care teams being set up, but it wasn't like that back then.

And anyway; break the word down and what do you have?

The rapist(s)

That's right. You can virtually rape a child emotionally by asking the wrong question at the wrong time, and leading questions are not allowed.

This is such a tricky area to manoeuvre around and in, made more difficult by feeling that you are working with your hands tied behind your back and your shoe laces are tied together so you may trip up at any time...then where would you be and, more importantly, what damage may you inadvertently cause to the child.

It was mostly left to me to log things and Julia to listen to me and keep me reassured that we were doing everything we could, as was she.

When we had decided to become foster carers we had attended the Choosing to Foster training.

This had involved attending weekly meetings over a course of six weeks.

Being naive we had thought we'd be caring for children that had been hit or not fed properly.

The training had opened our eyes to the very real fact that people actually hurt their children in ways that the average person just didn't imagine.

We had never really considered that an adult could find pleasure in thumping children or that an adult would find a child sexually exciting.

Even with the training, as eye opening as it was, it was basic, never prepared us for the reality of a child disclosing that they had been sexually abused.

I think for the average person nothing could ever prepare them because it is just too awful to comprehend.

Jenny and Chloe weren't the first children to have disclosed such horrors to me.

On reflection, some of their behaviours were blatantly similar to those of previous children that had gone through similar horrors, though some were more subtle.

I knew we would all come through this, I also knew I needed more training in the area of child sexual abuse, but unlike today when ongoing training is almost mandatory once you have been approved as a foster carer, back then it was quite sporadic and I almost felt a bit perverted even asking to attend training for this specific topic.

And then of course, you had to wait for a training opportunity to arise as social services couldn't and still can't provide all the training courses that their foster carers want and need, due to time constraints, venue and funding issues.

There just isn't the money in their budget to fund everything for everyone and if I remember correctly, HIV and drug awareness were the 'in' training needs at that time, all very important, just not to me and the children I was trying to care for at that time.

By now, it seemed pretty obvious that Jenny had been through some level of sexual abuse, and, possibly so had Chloe.

Julia decided we should try to do a disclosure interview with the police.

Nowadays, disclosure interviews tend to be carried out at special units and videotaped, back then they were held, it would appear, anywhere.

So 'anywhere' for this interview was to be my lounge, after school on a Friday afternoon.

On the morning of the interview Jenny and Chloe had sat on the floor facing each other after breakfast.

They were still in their nightdresses and their feet were touching.

Jenny pulled her nightdress up, stretching her legs apart as she did so, exposing herself to Chloe.

When Chloe copied her Jenny said she was being rude.

I told Jenny she was being naughty and took them to their room to get ready for the day.

I was just glad the interview was going to be done now and we may then have a bit more evidence to work with.

I made arrangements for my children to visit friends for tea and went to collect Jenny from school.

Timing is always important in fostering.

If you try to do a specific piece of work with a child too soon, disaster...but sometimes, just sometimes, a child plays the trump card.

On this day Jenny did just that.

Chapter 5

When I got to school, I was called into the office.

By now, her teacher and the headmistress, like me and Howard, were fairly concerned that Jenny had been sexually abused by someone and today Jenny had enforced this belief.

The headmistress handed me a box and explained that the children had been playing with plasticine this afternoon and Jenny had made a model that they thought I should see.

Inside the box was an unbelievably accurate plastercine penis.

The detail was very good (better than I could have done). I was gobsmacked and so upset because this little girl should not know what this part of the male anatomy looks like.

I slipped the model into my bag, collected Jenny and Chloe from my friend who had stayed with them in the playground, and went home, saying nothing to Jenny about what I had in my bag.

When we got home the police women arrived and were introduced as friends of Julia's.

Jenny and Chloe were drawing pictures and chatting away, not aware that the drawings could be used as part of the case that I hoped the police would be building against the bastards that had hurt these two young children.

Art can be very a useful tool in discovering some of the life events a child has experienced.

We had noticed that many of the children that shared our home would start off using only black pencils or crayons, gradually adding other colours as the weeks and months of security passed.

If they drew a picture of someone who had abused them they would usually omit the part of the body that had been used against them, so many had no arms or legs and some even had facial features missing.

The total joy of a child sharing our home that used bright colours from day one was a rarity.

I went into the kitchen with one of the policewomen and showed her the model.

I think, as much as it is upsetting, she was impressed with the detail, which is why I was so shocked by what happened to that seven inch piece of evidence.

This police woman took the model into the lounge and showed it to Jenny, telling her I'd been given it by the school.

This shocked me as I'd just told her Jenny didn't know I had it.

She then gave it to Jenny and asked what it was.

Jenny immediately squashed and rolled it up, laughing as she said 'it's a boat'.

One lost piece of evidence; one slightly damaged relationship.

Shit happens.

Chapter 6

Jenny's behaviour continued to bounce along, good, bad and indifferent.

However, she had now started to masturbate in front of me.

This started with her sitting on the floor with her legs at an almost impossible angle but getting her genital area in contact with the carpet (she had her underwear on at these times).

She would then just rock.

Because I was still quite naive, it took me some time to realise what she was doing and sort out diversionary tactics.

As soon as Howard or I noticed Jenny sitting in 'her comfort position' we would ask her to get something or come and play with us or the other children.

If we walked into the room and she was already rocking we would laugh and say something along the line of 'come on sweet heart, you'll wear a hole in the carpet' and scoop her up for a hug.

As time went on and she showed no sign of stopping, I had to reassure her that what she was doing wasn't naughty, just private.

I told her that if she needed to ease an itch, she should go to the bathroom or her bedroom.

I had to be very careful not to give this little girl another 'secret' to keep, I also had to make sure she didn't think she was dirty for having this need.

I can't for the life of me remember what I actually said, but fortunately she soon stopped wearing holes in the lounge carpet.

She did, however, discover a new way to reach her comfort zone in the company of others.

Jenny was always a very friendly child towards adults.

We noticed that when our male friends in particular (and oh my poor, poor father in law) came over to the house Jenny would always go to them for a cuddle.

And of course, our friends and family, knowing how needy these children were for kindness and attention; gave it to them by the bucketful...

At first, no-one was aware of how vulnerable they were, mostly because we couldn't tell them our concerns and, of course, most of our friends didn't foster and had no idea of the sort of abuse some families put their children through, though of course the media was slowly bringing child sexual abuse out into the open.

She would then sit on their lap chatting about whatever she had been up to for a few minutes, but remain on their laps while we chatted.

One day I noticed, as she sat on my father in laws lap that she was not sitting across, but had balanced herself astride one of his knees and was slowly rocking.

I could have died as I realised what she was up to!

I had to be careful so as not to embarrass my poor father in law as well as shift Jenny without making her feel bad about what she was doing.

Fortunately just then Edward, our eldest child living at home, came in and asked her if she wanted to play football with him and James in the garden and off she went.

Once the children were all in the garden, I explained to my father in law what she had been up to.

Poor man he was so embarrassed and shocked as he had no idea what these children had been through or witnessed in their short lives and to him, they were mere babies. They were little innocents who should know nothing of adult relationships and activities.

We knew from then on that if Jenny got onto anyone's lap for a hug, we would have to tell her to sit across both legs facing sideways.

This way she was not taking advantage of anyone and we hoped it would make her feel safer, as she may feel that our friends and family were actually abusing her in allowing this behaviour.

And so the time went on.

Both girls would periodically start singing about 'wibbly wobbly willies' or make some comment about the male genitalia.

One evening the children were all watching a children's programme on the television.

The programme was about baby animals.

A scene came on of a pig feeding her piglets and Chloe straight away started singing the 'wibbly willy' verse and Jenny joined in.

I later asked Jenny if the things she had told me had also happened to Chloe.

I wasn't sure if this was a leading question or not...I just needed to know more about their background if anyone was to be able to help them get over it.

Get over it isn't actually what happens though.

You come to term with events.

You learn to live with them.

You hope, with time, they will become such distant memories that are way outnumbered by the good memories you make as life continues.

Jenny said they had and that Chloe had cried like she had done herself.

She expanded to let me know that it had been in her room with the mat (though I never found out the relevance of the mat).

She also asked me if I would smack her granddad.

I told her that I would like to smack anyone who hurt her so she said I could smack her granny as well because she also licked her where her knickers went. This made me feel even more anger because, as wrong as it is for a man to abuse a child in such a way, for a woman to do so just seemed so much worse because they (we) are supposed to be the gentler sex, the caring and nurturing sex. A mother or grandmother should be there to protect and hold the child safe from harm...I know a dad and grandfather should as well, but historically men have been seen as more abusive and possibly less caring...perhaps that is a bit harsh of me. What I mean is...they are just masculine and as such; don't appear as gentle and caring.

She then said I could smack her uncle Paul because he hurt her, but she managed to run out of the house with no knickers on.

Her uncle called her back but her granddad had shut the door in her face.

Jenny told me that to punish her for running away her granddad put his hands where her knickers go and hurt her.

It seemed as though these poor children had no one to protect them and lived in a house full of demons.

I wasn't aware at that time the total relevance of 'a house full of demons'...

No wonder we were going through our own living hell with their behaviour, but as yet I was only concerned and upset for them.

Within the next few months I would become scared, really scared, for the safety of my children as well.

There was an upside to one discussion I had with Jenny.

She had been chatting about granddad and Uncle Paul, telling me they had willies, when I asked if she knew anyone else with a willy.

She just looked at me confused, and said 'no'.

When Howard came home from work that evening I laughed to him and said 'I'm so glad you haven't got a willy'.

He looked at me puzzled and asked what I was talking about.

I explained that Jenny didn't appear to understand that all men were built the same.

She'd obviously never seen his or the boys, therefore they didn't have one.

Thank goodness for safe care guidelines and our own modesty.

One day Jenny complained about being sore between the legs so I took her to the doctor.

We had a lovely doctor and, being male Jenny was very tactile with him.

This doctor was my all time favourite when any of our children needed to visit the surgery; home grown or borrowed, as he had the most wonderful manner with children, specializing in paediatrics.

He was also the police surgeon, getting called out to attend suspicious deaths and accidents.

She told him that her grandparents and uncle hurt her bottom so he referred her to the local hospital paediatrician for examination.

He said she appeared to be extremely mentally disturbed and in need of professional help.

Thank you doctor...with his support I could now ask Julia for some more in-depth support, and she could justify asking her bosses for it.

Jenny was still wetting the bed on an almost nightly basis.

Sometimes she would soak the bed twice in a night and keeping our home fresh smelling was a growing concern.

One morning I asked her if she would like me to get some special big girl nappies for her and she said she would, so I popped to the shops and got the biggest nappies I could find.

I told Jenny she didn't have to wear them if she didn't want to, but that if she thought she may wet the bed, just ask for one at bedtime.

That night, after her story she asked if she could have her nappy on.

I was aware that there were draw backs to allowing her to wear a nappy, but also that regression to a 'safe' time in her life could be beneficial.

What I hadn't bargained on was that she would not only wet a nappy, but also soil it, climb into Chloe's bed and smear the mess all over her sheets and duvet!

Poor Chloe, young as she was, was mortified.

Thank goodness this was a rare occurrence, but it happened on several occasions and the whole house knew about it because of Chloe's wailing indignation.

I had also not made the connection that the first time she did this was on the morning that her mum was coming for her monthly visit.

When behaviours are so negative, one more slipping in the door can easily be overlooked.

It took time, but we learned to take a step back on an almost daily basis and assess the wider picture.

To see all the behaviours, or as many as we could remember, as symptoms of the problems we needed to help the children address.

During this visit their mum gave both girls lots of hugs and appeared to be reading them stories.

I made sure she wasn't on her own with them and made excuses that they liked Howard to give them a bedtime story with our children.

She said goodnight to them and stayed downstairs when they went up, remaining downstairs with Howard when I went to tuck them in and put Jenny's nappy on.

Once the girls were in bed their mum sat chatting about her life.

She said she adored her dad but not her step mother because of what she had done, but didn't go into detail.

She told us that she spent most of her childhood in care and talked about her partner, who was the brother of a previous boyfriend that was due out of prison in the near future.

She didn't know what was going to happen then, especially if she had her children back as the brothers were discussing doing a 'job'.

Again no more detail.

It was very frustrating trying to keep up with the conversation she was having because it was like, lots of different conversations rolling into one and no real start or finish to any of them.

It made me think that if her life was as chaotic and jumbled as her talking, she had little hope realistically, of ever being able to parent her children appropriately and keep them safe.

What a relief when she finally left and we could be alone for a few minutes before the inevitable night time routine of traipsing up and down the stairs to Jenny and Chloe as they got in and out of bed or just cried out in their sleep. The positive of this was that I never needed to join a gym as I got so much running exercise and did plenty of weight lifting when we had wet beds.

But I digress, because we learnt an important lesson that night and, no matter how innocent an action looks, check again and keep your ears open as well as your eyes.

Chapter 7

The children settled as well as they usually did; they yo-yoed in and out of bed, cried and banged around and generally tired me out.

The only thing different tonight was that they were both getting very upset about spiders.

I couldn't see any spiders in their room.

In fact I couldn't see a spider in the house.

I asked Edward and James if they had been teasing Jenny and Chloe, not that I really thought they had because it wasn't their way, but I had to ask.

The next day both Jenny and Chloe became hysterical if they saw anything remotely resembling a spider and were driving me mad with their constant screaming and running to me because I didn't understand what was going on.

This behaviour continued on and off for weeks then suddenly stopped.

Peace, of a sort, at last.

Chapter 8

One weekend we decided to take the children to visit friends of ours who lived in Norfolk.

We had recently bought a new car with seven seats so travelling didn't present a problem anymore for our growing family.

We got up early and after breakfast and the inevitable bed changing, set off.

Our two sons sat in the back row of seats, Jenny, Chloe and Claire sat behind Howard and me and off we went.

I was driving, Jenny was behind me.

We had gone about twenty miles when Jenny said she felt sick, then, without further warning she threw up.

I never knew a child could spew so much.

As soon as she said she felt unwell, Howard had emptied the plastic bag containing travel nibbles in order for Jenny to use because I couldn't pull over immediately.

Jenny threw up all over his arm and, for the life of me I don't know how she did it, but she managed to get Chloe, Claire, Edward and James as well!

I was the only one in the car that was puke free.

Of course then all the children started to feel sick and so did the adults, which wasn't a good sign for the rest of the journey.

We had by now reached a small village and pulled into a garage forecourt that had a shop attached to it.

Everyone bundled out of the car and, because I was the only one not covered in puke and smelling so awful, I went in and bought some baby wipes so I could help get everyone cleaned up.

People are very kind when they see you have a problem and I managed to jump the queue as well as being given some paper towel to wipe up the larger amounts of wet goo.

I also bought some very strong car air freshener, but it took weeks to get rid of the smell even after giving the car several good washes.

The good thing was Jenny must have emptied out as she managed to complete the rest of the journey with no more mishaps.

The bad thing was, thanks to the smell in the car, everyone else was hanging on to their stomach contents for the rest of the journey.

We had a great day out and even managed to laugh about being chucked up over, which we still do to this date when reminiscing about this placement.

By the time we left the children were all falling asleep so, though we were well armed with plenty of plastic bags, they were not needed on the return journey home.

The smell in the car though meant that if one of the children woke, they may well be ill...I certainly felt like I could be at any time.

The girls' behaviour yo-yoed up and down as the days passed.

They had now started to play with their food if they were upset or angry and we had some food fights at meal times, with food literally flying across the table at everyone.

We soon learned to judge the children's moods and if they appeared to be in 'food-fight' mode they ate before everyone else which, though not ideal, meant the rest of the family could eat in peace.

Our children, for their part, never complained about the girls though must have felt extremely cross and upset at times.

Edward and James were quite protective 'big brothers and Claire looked out for Jenny as best she could while at school, bearing in mind she was just a year older.

One day, many months away, Howard and I were to be amazed at the commitment our young children had towards Jenny and Chloe and the sacrifice which they would jointly make in order to give them, what they thought was total security and a safe home.

Chapter 9

We were now four months into this placement, though it felt like the children had been with us a lifetime.

Jenny was still wetting her panties and soiling at school, but she had made a few friends and behaved very well when invited to their homes for tea.

It is always awkward when you have 'borrowed' children that attend pre-school or school and they have quite severe behaviour problems both in and out of our home.

You are obviously bound by the rules of confidentiality, yet also have a duty to protect other children from risk of any abuse that this child can inflict on them.

I had to make sure the parents were aware that they should be vigilant when Jenny was in their charge, explaining that she had a tendency to be accident prone and may hurt herself so was always supervised in whatever she was doing, while at the same time try not to damage her friendships by making the parents wary of having her in their homes.

This seemed to work as she continued to get invites and no complaints ever came back about her behaviour.

The nights were still being disturbed with both children crying without waking, or waking and wandering around.

They had also now taken to sharing their behaviours, in that one day Jenny would wet the bed and Chloe would wet the floor and the next day swap around.

This was frustrating to say the least and I think I shocked both children, and our own, when I finally blew and shouted that enough was enough and they had to try at least, to use the bathroom.

They promptly obeyed and started piddling over the bathroom carpet.

Such is life.

James and Claire, who were both prolific readers started to read stories to Jenny and Chloe if their behaviour started to become negative as they discovered it was an activity that would keep them engrossed for quite long periods of time.

Whether this was a control thing or not for Jenny and Chloe, my children were doing something they enjoyed and I was getting a bit of peace and quiet.

Nothing was being broken or trashed while they sat and listened to a story.

I had always enjoyed cooking and our home had, until the arrival of Jenny and Chloe, been full of the smell of baked cakes but this had lapsed due to being unable to leave the girls unsupervised for any length of time.

I grabbed these spare moments to whip up some home baking for everyone, though gradually this tapered out and I had to concede to buying from local shops and a lovely man who did home delivery for all things sweet that children (and Howard) love.

Before we knew it another month had passed and contact day arrived.

I never told Jenny and Chloe about contact until the day as I knew they would play up and their behaviour would deteriorate.

Having said that; children seemed to have an inbuilt timer and they just knew when certain events were due, even if not the exact day it was due.

Once they had woken up, I told them their mum would be here this afternoon.

Both seemed pleased about this but within half an hour they were pinching and biting each other and this continued until Jenny went to school.

Chloe was good as gold all day but was very listless and couldn't settle to anything.

When their mum arrived they both ran to greet her, and then played up for the entire time she was here.

They were given new Wish Bear teddies which they cuddled for a few minutes then threw onto the floor.

After cuddling up to their mum for a while Jenny said 'I'm going to cuddle mummy' and came to sit with me.

Throughout contact Jenny and Chloe then went over the top in calling me mummy.

They began and ended each sentence with the word mummy and only reacted if I answered.

It was clear something was going on between the girls.

We were used to being called mummy and daddy by the children that lived here because, though they were always given our names and told they could either call us aunty and uncle, or if they preferred, just our Christian names, most little ones copied our children, just not when they were seeing their birth parents.

Susan was clearly not amused by Jenny and Chloe's antics and, to be honest, I was finding it quite embarrassing because we always answered the children when they spoke to us.

Now, I didn't know for sure who they were talking to and only responding if they ignored responses made by Susan.

At the end of contact we allowed their mum to tuck them in and give them their story, though this was supervised.

Within five minutes of their mum leaving our home both girls were screaming at each other.

I went to settle them in bed again and, as I went upstairs I heard Chloe shouting 'She's *my* mummy,

Susan's yours' and Jenny was crying back 'No, she's *mine,* Susan's yours'.

I sat with them and reassured them they were staying here and that we were both of their parents while they lived here, because we are their foster parents (we could be that back then, not like now when we have to be known as foster carers).

I had taken up their new teddies for them to cuddle, thinking that maybe a new toy that their mother had given them would keep them happy.

Instead both had thrown them out of the bedroom and refused to have them returned. It would be a little while before we found out the secret of these teddy bears. They finally settled and went to sleep.

By ten o clock Chloe had drenched her bed and woke up screaming, taking some time to settle down again.

The following morning they threw their new teddies into the toy box and buried them under everything else.

These were beautiful little teddy bears; both children liked cuddling toys, so what was going on?

Even telling them the magic of the Wish Bear stories was to no avail.

I hadn't heard their mum say anything negative to them and had been in the room throughout the contact, but clearly something was amiss.

As with the last contact, it would be a while before I clocked on to what was going on, but when I did, contact at our home was stopped as the children had to know they were safe and no-one could hurt them while they were with us.

What I still had to learn was that, as much as I could reassure the children they were safe, I would soon need some reassurance that we all were.

Chapter 10

Following this contact the girls' behaviour regressed even more than usual.

The children argued and fought over everything and anything.

Mealtimes were like a war zone and bedtimes a total nightmare, with Howard cuddling one or other to sleep in the lounge late at night as I stayed up getting the ever increasing pile of laundry washed and ironed.

Jenny became even more vacant and wandered around in an almost trance like state when she was home and unless I stood directly in front of her when speaking she appeared neither to see me nor hear me.

If we went to the park the children became very clingy and tearful meaning these little excursions had to be stopped and visiting friends was impossible as they would both wet themselves and become fretful.

If I had a meeting to attend or one of the rare training days I knew there would be repercussions if this encroached in to any part of the day that I would normally spend with the children.

They were used to me either being home with them or collecting them from play school and school.

If I was otherwise detained and had my parents or Howard's parents collect the children and look after them for a short time they would invariably wet or soil the carpets in their homes and then play up once we got home.

Unfortunately review meetings cannot be dictated by children's behaviours and are a very important part of the work we do as it is the main forum for information sharing as well as decision making.

We took the support for granted as our parents were always willing to help in any way they could, but on reflection I'm sure they must have dreaded some of the babysitting they were asked to do, but still did so without complaining.

Understandably our parents were concerned about the very real danger of Jenny or Chloe accusing them of hurting them, though they continued to treat them as they treated every child that shared our home.

They treated them as their grandchildren.

Nothing more and nothing less.

A positive was that both Jenny and Chloe started to tell me little snippets of information that was starting to explain their behaviours.

I was told that the police had taken their granny away and that Susan had told them that she would let the police come here to take them away (this took a huge amount of reassurance that it wouldn't happen).

They also explained their mum had told them she would take them to their granddads house which seemed to terrify them both.

When I asked if it was a good or bad house Jenny said it was a bad one, not like here which was good.

Jenny's behaviour became quite alarming one day when a friend came with her little girl.

The children had been playing quite nicely in the garden. They hadn't argued or done anything to cause concern when suddenly Jenny jumped at the little girl, putting her hands around her throat and actually tried to strangle her.

For a moment Jenny's face was a picture of rage, though as quick as this look came on, it went.

She didn't seem to understand that it was very naughty and dangerous to put your hands around someone's throat.

Almost as quickly as she jumped at this little girl, she went back to playing as though nothing had happened.

As a rule I didn't leave the girls unsupervised for more than a flying visit to the loo, now I knew we had to be even more vigilant than ever if we had young children around.

Chapter 11

Just before their next contact I'd had a meeting to attend at the social services offices.

My friend Elizabeth, another foster carer, looked after Chloe at her home while Jenny was at school.

Elizabeth told me that when the washing machine repair man had arrived Chloe had walked straight up to him and asked him if he was going to hurt her.

The poor man apparently looked quite concerned. He became even more so when a little later Chloe asked him if he was going to kill her.

I had never heard Chloe speak like this before and was naturally concerned myself at the content of this little conversation, though Chloe never made any reference to it again.

A few days later Howard went into the girls' bedroom to collect the wet bedding.

Jenny was squatting on the floor and when Howard asked what she was doing she told him she wanted to go to the toilet.

She was sent to the bathroom where she promptly peed over the floor.

Later, while at school she did the same in the library though this time she soiled herself as well.

I was called into the office before the children came out of their class and told about this episode. It was clear that the head and Jennies teacher were tired of her behaviour and at a loss, as was I, as to what actions to take next in order to help her move forward.

Once we got home I tried speaking with Jenny again about what was nice behaviour and what wasn't.

Jenny just ignored me, looking through me as though I wasn't there. Having tried several different approaches in dealing with the behaviours these children gave, I finally blew.

I told Jenny off very sternly and told her that it was time she started to make an effort to get on with people and to behave if she was to live with us happily.

I was now more than a bit concerned that the school could refuse to have her attend and in all honesty, they would have been justified in their actions had they taken this route.

To date I hadn't heard of a child crawling around the and room in the school trying to empty their bowels and now it seemed most of the other parents did, as their children had excitedly told them at the end of the school day.

Jenny was now disrupting not only our home life, but the education of her class mates. I was so aware that other parents could ask that Jenny be excluded. I wouldn't have blamed them but don't know how I would have coped had anyone taken that course of action. I guess we were fortunate that exclusions then, unlike now, were a rarity and not something your average parent thought about.

I couldn't afford to have her home all the time as she needed to be educated and I needed the space that the school day afforded me.

I so desperately needed that time either alone or just with Chloe when she wasn't at pre-school.

I seemed to be spending all my time praying that my support network would remain intact and that we would get additional help, though where from I didn't know, to support the children with their problems and behaviours which seemed to grow almost by the day.

Jenny and Chloe's behaviour had just about settled down when it was contact day again.

As usual I waited until the day before mentioning it.

This time I got no reaction.

No negative behaviour, no fighting and no screaming.

Breakfast went fine with five children boisterously eating and chatting about whatever it is that children talk about and then everyone getting ready for school and off we went.

After school I had a bit of shopping to do and Claire was leaving school late so we didn't get home until four o clock, which hadn't appeared to bother Jenny and Chloe at all.

They had quietly walked around the shops and walked slowly home even though they knew their mum would be waiting on the door step.

As we neared our home they just said 'Oh look, mums here', seeming pleased but cautious.

Knowing the probable reaction to contact, I just wished Susan hadn't made the effort to get to our home from hers, which I knew was quite a trek and involved several trains and buses.

Once we got indoors Susan had to ask for a cuddle, which she was quickly given, then I was given a huge hug.

Susan then started playing a game with them where she tipped them upside down. If they said they loved her most she tipped them the right way, if they didn't she left them upside down.

The whole contact was spent with Susan asking if they loved her and Susan saying 'Mummy loves you lots'.

It was a very strained contact to say the least as both children were definitely playing me and their mother off against one another.

At no time during this contact were the children alone with their mother, yet once again at bedtime they became extremely upset and cried for nearly two hours, saying they wanted to stay with us and not go back to their granddads house.

They both needed so much reassurance through the night, not only from me but also from Howard, which was a stress step up from other contact nights. At least I could try to catch a few minutes rest throughout the following day, but poor Howard would have to put in a full day of work in the office while he felt fit for nothing but sleep.

What on earth could have happened this time?

Over the years we have learnt that children in the care system have many survival techniques.

One of these is the ability to hear a conversation from fifty feet away and behind closed doors.

Once the children were in bed Susan told us that she was now a Mormon and was staying with a friend of hers.

She was applying to the courts for more contact with the children and was getting beds for them so they could have overnight stays leading up to them returning to live with her.

But of course, we didn't know then that Jenny and Chloe may have heard this conversation as they were tucked up in bed at the front of the house, while we were chatting at the back of the house downstairs.

As usual, their behaviour following contact digressed and became more concerning.

Night terrors were now the norm for them, with them crying without waking and bed wetting almost nightly and sometimes twice a night.

Fortunately I've always been a shopaholic for all things to do with children and had bought plenty of pretty girlie duvet sets so at least their bedroom always looked nice, though keeping it smelling nice was another matter.

The weather was also improving so windows could be left open all the time and having secondary double glazing meant the children were all safe because the inner pane was locked shut at the end where the big window was open, so at least our home didn't smell of urine.

Jenny and Chloe now woke most mornings between five and five thirty.

They were still sharing a room with Claire at this time but luckily she was a heavy sleeper and they didn't disturb her very often.

When they did she would come into our bed leaving Jenny and Chloe to play in the bedroom.

Jenny and Chloe also started to sing nursery rhymes.

They would sing them over and over again, getting faster and faster until they muddled all the words up.

Both would be openly defiant and refuse to listen to everyone, even having a story read to them now held little interest.

One night Chloe screamed out, when I went to her she was still asleep, holding herself between the legs and kicking out at something or someone that was invisible.

This was to be a recurring event for several weeks to come.

Another night, when I went to check the children and cover them before I went to bed Jenny lashed out at me and thumped the quilt for a few minutes before settling.

She hadn't woken up at this time and I had been quite surprised at the strength and violence in her little fist.

Jenny had also become quite pre-occupied with 'poo'.

If anyone went to the toilet she wanted to know if they had 'been'.

This became a source of great irritation for Edward and James who, until then had been very protective but now started to distance themselves a little.

Jenny was also still soiling herself one or two times a day.

Thank goodness the school were so supportive because I think they would have been quite justified in asking that she be kept home until this problem had resolved itself.

Perhaps, like me, they knew this problem couldn't 'resolve' itself.

I don't think, in all the years we have had borrowed children sharing our home and using that primary school, I have ever known more commitment to a child or support for my family than I had at that time.

There are no words that could ever express my total gratitude to the staff that helped me without even knowing how much they were doing at the time.

Chloe had now started to copy Jenny with the vacant looks.

Talking to her was very difficult as she just looked through you. I wondered if this beautiful and responsive child might be epileptic, though there had been no signs before the vacancies she now had. And of course, these vacancies tended to coincide with a request for her to do something as opposed to being random episodes.

I guessed she was doing what Jenny did. She was taking herself off to some safe place inside her head where no-one and no-body could reach her or hurt her.

She cried through most nights without waking and was fretful through the days because she was so tired.

I was exhausted with the constantly disturbed nights and trying to comfort a child all day without knowing why she needed the comfort, making it hard to know if I was doing right or wrong.

Levels of spite were escalating as well.

My niece, having suffered at the girls hands before still chose to play with them, such is the innocence of children and their high level of forgiveness.

My niece was only two years old but didn't want to be held and cuddled by Jenny so Jenny hit her hard across the face leaving an ugly red mark.

Later she managed to slam the lid of the toy box on Sarah's hand and arm.

Chapter 12

By now I had discovered that during contact in my home their mother had whispered things to them.

She had whispered very important and controlling things. She had whispered nasty and terrifying little messages from their granddad.

Over the course of the past few weeks, Jenny and Chloe had told me about how powerful their granddad was.

It was funny how they started to speak.

First it was a whisper, very quietly and only when we were out of the house.

They would usually ask if I could see a spider or a fly.

If I laughed and said yes they would become quiet.

If I said no they would tell me that granddad knows everything.

I quickly learnt what response to use.

It turned out that their mother had told them at the first contact not to say anything about their grandparents because they were being watched. They were being watched by *every* fly and spider that passed them by and even the ones they didn't see...saw them.

These poor children just *knew* that their granddad would know everything they said and did because the flies and spiders would be reporting back to him.

How nasty is that?

But to make things even worse, and without even realising how I was being dragged into this abusive behaviour, they were then given the teddy bears which Susan had asked me to encourage them to cuddle as it would make her feel like they were closer to her if she knew they were loving the toys she had given them.

I had encouraged the children to love and cuddle these toys.

I had been duped into becoming a granddad supporter without even knowing it!

Jenny and Chloe knew what I didn't, that these teddy bears were special because they could communicate with granddad.

They would let granddad know everything the girls said and did and do it with my support.

How dare she treat me like this! How dare any of that family!

How dare anyone drag me into their depraved little world!

As it happened though, the teddies had been thrown out of the toy box one day and both girls had set about trying to rip them up.

I had taken them away and told Jenny and Chloe that I would put them in a cupboard until they wanted to play nicely with them.

Jenny and Chloe never saw those teddies again, as one day; shortly after discovering how 'powerful' they were I gave them to a local jumble sale...

No-one, no matter how deviously they tried, was going to hurt a child in my home if I had anything to do with it!

I would be speaking with their social worker to ask if Jenny and Chloe's contact with Susan could either be cancelled all together or held in the contact suite.

It had become quite clear now that Susan was still abusing her daughters while she was visiting them in our home.

If this continued, in Jenny and Chloe's minds our home may no longer be a safe place for them...worse...they may lose what little trust they had in us if they thought we were becoming, or had always *secretly* been part of their past.

Chapter 13

It was in June, five months into this placement that we started to make progress and get more information on their early years from Jenny and Chloe.

Jenny had woken up in an unhappy and antagonistic mood and had been like this through breakfast and all the way to school.

Chloe had been quite happy throughout the day, playing nicely with her toys and me or helping with little household chores, but this ended when we got home after picking the children up from school in the afternoon.

If Chloe was playing on the floor Jenny would walk over and stand on her hands or any part of her that she chose.

She had also slammed the toilet door on Chloe's hand when she had tried to get into the bathroom.

I had to stop preparing the evening meal and sit with Jenny.

I asked her why she was being so naughty and she burst into tears.

Jenny begged me not to tell her granddad she was being naughty because he would hurt her.

I asked her if the things she said he had done had been punishments and she said they had.

She was now sobbing on my lap, shaking and saying she didn't want to go back to granddad because he was naughty and hurt her bottom.

She said he hit her and put his finger in her bottom.

I had to stay calm and consider the questions I needed her to answer, but knew if I took too long she would stop talking again. Also, I wanted this over before Edward, James and Claire came back into the room, and felt grateful that they had started to spend more time with each other in the boy's bedrooms than downstairs with Jenny and Chloe.

When I asked if anyone else did this she said her Uncle Paul.

I sat holding Jenny and giving her as much reassurance as I could while I tried to get my mind around what this little girl was saying.

This was not the first time we had worked with child victims of sexual abuse and no doubt it wouldn't be the last, but it hurt.

Every time a child disclosed such abuse it hurt me so much.

I knew that with each new disclosure I would have difficulty getting much needed sleep as every time I closed my eyes I would see the child reaching out to safety and I just couldn't quite reach them.

Worse still, sometimes it was my own beautiful children that would be crying for me to help them.

I would then lay in bed, tears running down my cheeks, hoping Howard wasn't aware of my distress in case he said enough was enough, knowing he would be concerned at how I was coping with everything that was going on around us.

It is only with hindsight that I know Howard was aware of my distress. Howard, in his own gentle and kind way, supported me through it all. What a quietly strong man I had married. It was me sadly, too wrapped up in the children's and my own emotional traumas, that was unaware of his distress or what support he may have needed.

It hurt like hell to think that anyone could get any pleasure from hurting children in any way.

Once Jenny had calmed down a bit she told me that she smacked her granddads bottom with his trousers up then down and her granddad laughed, but she didn't like it when he did the same to her because it hurt.

Jenny said that her granddad hurt her bottom one day before putting her coat on her and saying he was going to put her in a home.

Her dad came and she stayed with him until her granddad took her back, hurt her again and hit her hard.

Jenny was very sullen and spoke quietly at this time.

It was as if the life was being sucked out of her and she was just this tiny little scrap of a child who it seemed had had nowhere and no-one to run to.

The following day passed uneventfully.

Then, at bedtime Chloe asked for a sweetie.

I laughed and reminded her that we don't have sweets at bedtime.

Chloe looked at me with her beautiful big blue eyes and said that granddad gave her sweeties at bedtime but they weren't nice.

She explained her granddad was a naughty man and she hit him, but not her nanny.

Jenny then came into the bedroom and repeated what Chloe had said, that granddad and Uncle Paul were both naughty to them.

I asked Jenny if everything she'd told me they had done to her, they had done to Chloe and she said they had.

At this time Jenny also told me that her 'self' was hurting (this is what she called her vagina) and asked me to put some cream on her.

I had already learnt that with children above the age of about twenty months it was best to show them how to apply creams and lotions to their genital areas so as not make them feel we are in any way abusing them.

Another sad realisation, as we had naively come into fostering to care for children who had not been fed properly or had been smacked too hard.

We'd had quite a learning curve so far and as each child left Howard and I would look at each other, smile and say 'Well, things can only get better after that'.

And to be honest, with only one exception, we didn't have a sadder, more depraved, emotionally draining and physically exhausting placement ever again after Jenny and Chloe left.

Having said that we still had all the trauma of similar cases to work with, just the terrifying sadistic evilness of this case was missing, so though my bible is always by my bed, I no longer have to have it open at Psalm 83:18 'So let them learn that thou alone art Lord, God Most High over all the earth'.

To non-believers this may sound a trifle pathetic, but for me, a daily reminder that *my* God is always right beside me and will help whenever I ask was and is a great comfort, even though the way he helps isn't always clear at the time.

Chapter 14

As we went towards the end of June Chloe started to display ever more concerning behaviours.

She had been, since arriving in our home a beautiful little 3 year old girl that everyone had taken to.

She could light up a room with her smile and was so affectionate that everyone wanted to give her a hug.

Now she was waking up more often through the night and just crying as she stared into space.

During the day she bounced between being just totally adorable to absolute nightmare, filled with raging anger and tears.

She did not always have the words to explain what was going on in her mind, for that was the only place things could be 'going on' as her everyday life was so 'predictable'.

Our routine was taking the children to school then Chloe either went to play school, visited a friend or we came home and spent the day playing together or Chloe would 'help' me with the housework.

It was the middle of the week when Chloe had one of her bad nights.

Howard and I had been out during the evening to see a school production that the older children were in.

When we got home, my parents, who had babysat, told us they had been up and down all evening to Chloe but all she'd done was cry and say nothing. My poor parents were left feeling as frustrated and helpless as we were in comforting her.

I spent the rest of the evening up and down the stairs, deciding that our next move would be to a bungalow as this was too much exercise in one night.

Chloe finally settled at one o clock in the morning and I crashed out as well.

After Chloe and I had taken the children to school the next morning we went home.

I was too tired today for any stops in the park or visiting friends, I just wanted to lie on the settee and doze while Chloe played near me.

Chloe had other plans though.

Once we got home I made us a drink and lay on the settee.

Chloe came and sat with me and we had a little cuddle. Mmmm, play my cards right and we would both have a little sleep, tucked up together on the settee.

Just talk quietly, soothingly, drowsily...

I quietly asked Chloe if she felt better today after all the crying she had done last night.

Chloe told me that she'd had a bad dream. Oh no...I'm just too tired for this.

I figured that if I asked Chloe questions in a dozy voice she may start to feel sleepy herself, so I asked in my most sleepy voice who was in the dream and she said "Granddad".

"He was talking up my nightie and Jenny's nightie".

Ok...now I am like *wide awake*! What is it with these girls and their timing?

Well, Chloe certainly had my attention now and I guessed I'd be getting little sleep this evening either because jenny and Chloe would be having night terrors, or I would!

I asked Chloe if he had hurt her while talking up her nightie but she said he wouldn't hurt her.

Chloe was now firmly sat on my lap with little intention of going to play with any toys.

Her little legs were clamped tightly together and she was almost rigid.

Chloe then told me that grandma and her nightie were also in her dream and granddad hurt her up her nightie and kissed her on the mouth and legs.

Though Chloe was very close to tears at this time I presumed that she meant granddad had hurt her grandma and not her, because she was quite adamant that he wouldn't hurt her.

Time would tell though and as we had at least half of every day alone together, it meant we had started to form quite a nice bond and I knew, slowly, this lovely little girl was starting to trust.

Not that she trusted the police of course.

That was something we had to work on fairly quickly as we had a very active police presence in our community and I had always encouraged all 'our' children to speak to the 'nice policeman/woman'.

The first time we met up with the beat bobby we were on our way home from school in the morning.

Chloe was chattering away as usual when all of a sudden she went silent as she spun from walking beside me holding my hand, to being in front of me and burying her face in my shirt.

I managed not to fall over her and asked what on earth was wrong.

Chloe told me that the police were bad and that they wanted to kill her.

It took quite a bit of time and patience to convince both the girls that the police are good and that if ever they needed help, they should look for a policeman.

It was around this time that I got my first positive about Jenny from her teacher.

I had gone to collect her from her class at the end of the day when I was told that she had been showing her 'willy' to the children during lunchtime.

Although this wasn't *the* positive, it was followed by the comment that, on the whole, although academically she is well behind, emotionally she appears to be settling well and behaves herself for much of the time.

I was really pleased to know that, but concerned that she was now showing her genitals off to everyone in the playground.

Jenny had stopped soiling and wetting almost daily now so for that, at least, the school was pleased.

Chapter 15

As we slipped into July Jenny started to wet herself at school on an almost daily basis.

Her teacher was still taking a change of clothes in to school every day and I was sending in changes for Jenny.

The laundry, which I did most days, was now being done at a rate of up to five machine loads a day and the pile of ironing never seemed to diminish.

With five children and two adults normal weekly wear and bedding, we then had one or two wet beds a night as well as however many changes of clothes Jenny managed to go through a day.

The girls had also started to touch each other intimately and though they had both been told this was wrong, they showed no sign of embarrassment over their actions, indeed, being quite open about it.

Chloe was also getting a bit aggressive towards Jenny, kicking her as she walked past and one evening even kicked Jenny in the face as they were getting ready for bed.

It seemed as though the more confident Chloe became within our family and at her pre-school, the more aggressive she was getting, but only towards her sister.

Everyone adored Chloe with her ready smile and her huge eyes that were so beautiful when she was smiling, and as she was so very well behaved in front of visitors and friends, it was only family that saw how poor Jenny was now suffering behind closed doors.

At the same time Chloe was suffering because Jenny was very manipulative and was the main instigator in the sexual acts that went on between the girls, whether it was by verbal instruction or simple actions, Jenny tended to get Chloe to do whatever she wanted her to do and virtually, whenever she wanted it done.

This could be very frustrating as sometimes we would be ready to leave the house only to find Jenny and Chloe had both got back into their nightclothes and settled themselves back into their beds.

I didn't have to say anything to the girls about contact with their mother.

Most children within the care system, have an innate ability, to tell exactly where they are regarding contact and how many days have passed and when they are due to go again.

This appears to be irrespective of their age.

True to form, the behaviour deteriorated for a few days before contact was due to take place.

As I had voiced my concerns to Julia about what was being said to the girls it had been decided that contact would take place at a family centre.

This contact was to be with Susan and one of Jenny and Chloe's siblings, who was also being looked after within the care system, though living with a foster family quite a few miles away from where we lived.

Thankfully, this child had been taken into care at birth, so had not endured any of the abuse Jenny and Chloe had.

I know it sounds really nasty, but I was truly happy as we drove to contact and could put up with any amount of bad behaviour over the next week or so, because I knew this was to be the last contact for the girls with their mother.

Julia had spoken with other social workers that were involved with this family, as well as her manager about our concerns.

A meeting had been held and the decision to stop all future contact had been made.

We would however, at some future date, have to justify that decision.

She would never again be able to whisper scary messages to them or give them nightmares.

The department had asked me to explain to Jenny and Chloe that they would not be seeing their mother again after today.

So on the way we chatted and sang nursery rhymes as was usual when we were out in the car.

I chose this time, when I knew I had the children's attention, to tell them that this was a 'goodbye' contact.

Of course I couldn't just cheerfully say "No more mummy hurray", though felt like it.

Equally, I couldn't sound too upset or sad about it for fear of upsetting them and making them feel that maybe, just maybe, I was actually on 'mummies side'.

I simply told them that some very important people thought it would be nicer for them if they didn't see their mummy for a while so they could be happier and like their friends...just have one mummy and daddy that they live with all the time.

Both appeared to accept what I was telling them without concern.

We went to the offices before going to see their mother at the family centre.

Both girls seemed to be pleased to see their mother, though Chloe asked her who she was and what her name was.

The time spent with their mother was as usual noisy, though in different surroundings, they had a light meal and played with the toys.

After the contact Jenny and Chloe ran out of the building to come home and had to be called back to say goodbye to their mother, being reminded that they wouldn't see her again.

Jenny and Chloe sang nursery rhymes all the way home.

I was trying to keep everything as normal as possible until I got home, as I didn't want to have to cope with any major upsets while driving down country lanes.

Fortunately Chloe wasn't sick until we turned into our road, which was a bonus as Howard could sort the car out while I prepared our evening meal and caught up with what our children had been doing with the babysitter while I'd been out.

After the contact the girls settled very well to sleep, though Jenny had the morning off school the following day as she became upset because she thought she'd forgotten to say goodbye to her mother, though quickly settled when I reminded her that I had called her back after she'd run off the previous evening once contact had ended.

As Chloe was happy to go to play school, it meant I could give Jenny some undivided attention and reassurance that everything would carry on as it was, just that they wouldn't be seeing Susan again.

I deliberately used her name as I was by now aware that the plan for Jenny and Chloe was adoption.

Though how long that would take was anyone's guess.

If they carried on like they were at the moment they would leave our home as adults.

When I look back to how things were done years ago I can see so many great methods being stopped for the sake of 'political correctness', but there were also so many bad practices all done in the best interest of the child.

The department gave foster carers information to pass on to the child, but gave no advice as to the best time to do this. Also, sometimes a social worker would dob out of telling a child upsetting information because they didn't want the child to think they were responsible for stopping the child from doing something...better to let the child think it is the foster carers doing as this is the easier relationship to mend with the child living there.

Who in their right mind would actually tell children on the way to contact that this was it?

But as a naive 'fledgling' foster carer it was not my place to question a care plan, it was my place to do as I was asked by the 'professionals', and of course, suffer the consequences when the children played up if they didn't like what they were being told.

It was almost like foster parents were there just to do the dirty work.

Having said that, Julia was an excellent social worker, keeping me informed of everything that was going on behind the scenes with this placement.

Julia was also one of the rarer social workers who not only listened to what I said, but heard it as well.

Even nowadays this is quite rare, as social workers seem quite pre-occupied with their own agenda for each case and watching their own back, that irrespective of the information that foster carers give, plough straight ahead and 'do their own thing'.

This is such a great shame as local authorities up and down the country must be losing many good carers because of their inability to hear.

Some days after their last contact, Jenny overheard me talking to Julia.

That's another thing I've learnt about children in care.

They have this amazing hearing.

They can be in a different room, or even in the garden, but as soon as you think you can have a quiet word with a social worker about something you don't want to share with the kids just yet, their ears prick up.

Like radar they home in on you and know almost the whole content of any conversation within minutes.

The conversation was about the girls' care plan.

I knew already that the plan was for them to be placed with an adoptive family.

Jenny became very upset and cried that she didn't want a new mummy and daddy, she was staying here.

I spent some time reassuring her that no-one would ever just come and take her away.

I told her that most children, when they meet their forever mummy and daddy like them and actually ask if they can live with them.

We also talked about how she felt when she came to live with us, as at that time she didn't know what we were like and that must have been a scary time for her, but she had quickly settled in and become part of our family.

Jenny eventually calmed enough to go and play, though left me aware that there would have to be some work done to prepare her for a move at some time in the future.

We had also, early in the month been asked to have a new born pre adoption placement which was lovely as it meant, not only was I doing a bit of easy 'work' as there were no issues with a new born, but at some stage, I could use this baby as an example to explain to Jenny and Chloe about how lovely new mummies and daddies were.

But as with many things happening during the time Jenny and Chloe shared our home, even this little baby, who was so innocent, was going to invoke such memories for the children and lead to a very disturbing, stomach churning disclosure.

Chapter 16

It was around this time that Chloe started to concern me in the way she would play with our dog.

I will introduce you to the family 'mutt' here, as to have shared a brief part of his life was an experience!

David, the son I gained when I married Howard, was 9 years older than our eldest Edward.

Our three young ones adored their big brother and loved it when he came to see us. Claire was like a cling on and would invariably be found either stuck to his side on the settee or curled up on his lap. Poor David's girlfriends always got shunted out of the way when they visited as Claire was so possessive of her big brother.

One day early in December the year before, he and his girlfriend had asked if they could get the children a dog for Christmas.

Howard and I knew that the kids would love that so we said yes.

I went with David to see the dog he had chosen. I should have been suspicious at this point when this bouncing little dog was bought out of his kennel to see us but all I noticed was the state of the place and this lovely looking little dog.

It was at a dog rescue place and this dog was a small cross (not literally cross as in angry you know) terrier and something.

Anyway, David paid for the dog and we took it home.

The children were delighted with their early Christmas present and called the dog Lucky.

As it turned out the dog was damned lucky...lucky I didn't skin it and feed it to the local foxes!

Actually, he was a lovely little dog.

Turned out he was a cross between a terrier and a kangaroo. He was the only dog I ever met that could bounce so high he could lick the ceiling clean.

Sometimes it was as though he thought he was a bird and kept trying to sit on your shoulders - this when you were standing up.

After we'd had Lucky for a few weeks we decided to take him to a country local park.

Once there we let him off the lead and had the most energetic afternoon ever because he ran off down the hill and into the woods. No amount of calling got him to return.

We all ran after him and he kept stopping until we were about 100 yards away and then off he went again. That turned out to be the only time we ever let him off the lead as it took almost two hours of running after him, ignoring him and walking away from him before we managed to get hold of him and get his lead on.

One day I went out shopping, shutting the mutt in the kitchen (I say mutt with affection because we did all love this little creature). I closed the kitchen door, which was a bi fold one, placing the child safety gate behind it to prevent Lucky from opening it and wreaking havoc in the lounge.

What a waste of time.

As I approached the front garden on my return I thought something looked different about our home. I couldn't quite think what had made me feel uneasy, but I just knew something was amiss.

The front door was shut, but, something was wrong. I unlocked the door and as I did so I saw Lucky. I knew no-one else had a key and Howard was at work. How the hell had he got into the hall?

Then I saw what must have alerted me to a problem.

We had no curtains hanging at the windows (I was going through my 'no nets' phase at the time). All we had was curtain tapes with raggy bits of material hanging down here and there.

Lucky was already running into the lounge heading for the patio doors with his ears so flat to his head he didn't look like he had any.

Luckily I'm not into violence on living creatures so let him into the garden and thumped hell out of the feather cushions on the settee. Stupid dog thought he was Tarzan now!

But no matter how stupid Lucky could be he was very much loved by our family and the children who shared our home.

He was very protective of all the young ones and seemed to enjoy all the cuddles and affection he received (and he received lots, as he always wanted to be sitting on someone and be fussed over).

It was very sad to think that, this much loved dog, scatty animal that he was, would be our children's ultimate sacrifice for other children and the local authority.

I often wonder if social workers are really aware of what a family gives up for other people's children.

It is true that fostering families gain a tremendous amount from the work they do. To see a child smile after weeks of being sullen or withdrawn, to hear a child speak with feeling instead of a flat monotone and to have a child spontaneously wrap their arms around your neck and give you a quick hug, just because they can, is just brilliant.

The down side though is that, even as an adult, you learn that this world can be a very wicked place.

Your children learn as well.

Obviously we had to protect our young family from harm. As far as we were and still are concerned, protecting our children meant not only from physical harm, but also from the harm of information on or from the children that were placed with us.

I think we managed quite well and though we made sure our children knew that if any child placed with us asked them to keep a secret, or told them anything they were 'bothered' about, they were to tell us, our children fortunately were never the recipient of any disclosures from our borrowed children.

Chapter 17

One morning I came downstairs to see Chloe happily playing with the dog's genitals.

She clearly knew this was not a good thing to be doing as she stopped as soon as she saw me. Jenny was also in the room and sitting in her 'comfort' position.

This was a great start to the weekend, but what the hell, 'distract, distract, distract', had become our motto, and try to get the girls talking about whatever they had been through and what was going on in their heads.

Over the following few weeks I either saw Chloe playing with the dog's genitals, or one of our children would shout at her to leave the dogs bits alone.

Now we had to protect the dog from the children as well as protect them from the dog, because I'm sure the dog was getting some pleasure out of what was going on.

It got to the stage where the dog had to be wherever me or Howard was, which meant he spent quite a bit of time shut in the kitchen while I prepared meals, having the run of downstairs in the evenings once the little ones were in bed.

Because of the erratic behaviour Jenny and Chloe could display and the fact that, as a family, we desperately needed a break, it was decided that we would not take the girls away with us when we went on our annual holiday.

There was also the issue of where we were going.

We tended to spend all our holidays 'camping' on the moors in Devon. Our children thought this was great, the wild outdoors, no running water, no electricity, no proper loo and no shops.

We all enjoyed a total back to basic holiday with bathing in a freezing river and cooking fish finger sandwiches over a fire in the great outdoors. This was our little piece of heaven, our Utopia.

It would be the girl's worse nightmare...totally dark at night, no mod cons, no television, which would mean no light relief for anyone, surrounded by trees and, worse than anything else, we knew they would find spiders and all sorts of creepy bugs.

The last thing we wanted was to give them a holiday that they would never forget but for the wrong reasons.

It was lucky that Chloe was such a popular little girl and everyone loved her.

One day I happened to say to one of Chloe's play school teachers that we were not taking the girls away with us.

Anna asked if she and her family could look after them while we were on holiday. As I knew the family, we all attended the same church and our children went to the same school, I asked Julia if this would be okay.

The department agreed that it would be less upsetting for the children to spend the two weeks with people they knew already, and who could keep to a similar routine, including taking the children to church, so we started proper introductions with the children spending a few hours with our friends each week for two weeks before we went away.

The first time they did this, as they were leaving, Chloe asked Steve, Anna's husband if he was going to hurt her. Poor man wasn't aware of all the issues relating to these little girls and was terribly upset by the question, but reassured her that he wasn't.

When we got home both girls were very excited about going on holiday to Aunty Anna and Uncle Steve. What none of us realised was that this 'holiday' would prove to be the catalyst for a whole new hugely traumatic disclosure, which would mean a total rethink on what would be in the children's best interest as adoption was moved off the Richter scale.

During the first week of August Claire went away with the Brownies.

This gave me an ideal opportunity to rethink sleeping arrangements in our home.

I had walked into the girl's bedroom the day after Claire went to camp and found Jenny sexually abusing Chloe. I had become a little accustomed to the girls being overly tactile with each other but this was something else.

I asked Jenny why she was touching Chloe like she was and her response was "Granddad does", therefore totally normalising the behaviour. I asked Chloe if she liked what Jenny was doing and she said a definite "No".

I told Jenny that she mustn't touch Chloe any more, and told Chloe that if Jenny did this again she was to shout "Get your hands out my knickers!"

We woke many mornings to that little sentence being shouted out and me having to rush in to remind Jenny that she was not to do this, as well as having to run up the stairs at night to put Jenny back in her own bed.

Because of this it was decided that our sons would share a bedroom and Claire would have her own room, just in case Jenny tried to touch her while she was asleep.

We explained to Edward, James and Claire that it was because Jenny and Chloe had so many nightmares and they must be disturbing Claire even if she didn't actually wake up.

Fortunately this explanation was accepted by our children and the boys were happy to share. Claire was not so happy to give up her big bedroom, though saw the bonus of having her own space, albeit in a smaller bedroom.

Chloe had also now started to eat random items, ranging from any fluff on the carpet to breaking hangers into little pieces and popping them into her mouth.

Jenny was also becoming more obstinate in her behaviour.

She would now expose herself to our sons and anyone who came into our home.

With the bedroom to themselves they became quite loud and fairly destructive in the mornings, jumping on and over the furniture and shouting at the top of their voices.

Fortunately I'm the only light sleeper in our family and everyone else tended to sleep through the noise. Whether this was a cry for attention from them both because the baby had arrived or because they were not coming away with us I don't know, all I am certain of is that I was becoming desperate for a break.

The constant high level of supervision was knackering.

Trying to be positive towards the girls was becoming extremely hard work.

Knowing that many of the behaviours that children in care display are either learned negatives, protection or anger doesn't help much when you are assaulted on a daily basis and having to watch your children's bewilderment at the antics of these kids.

Then, three days before we were going on holiday, I walked into the lounge to see Jenny trying to pull the dog's face off.

Our poor little dog, who had gone through so much before he came to our home, was struggling to get away.

Jenny had her hands on either side of the dog's face, right by his eyes, and was pulling as hard as she could. Her right foot was under the dog's face and she was stretching her leg and leaning back to add weight to her efforts.

I was so shocked I actually shouted at her to "Let the dog go!"

The poor dog couldn't even whimper, well, to be honest I think he was having trouble breathing at that moment and even as she released him he could only manage to crawl away.

I checked he was okay and asked Jenny why she had tried to hurt the dog but she had no response. I was so very angry right at that moment and thought, just three days, if I can just get over the next three days everything will seem better when we get home and our batteries are recharged.

How wrong I was, yet again. How very, very, wrong I was.

The day before we went on holiday all the children were excited.

Our three played nicely and helped me by packing their favourite toys that were coming with us. It was quite a long journey so they also packed small activities for in the car.

Jenny and Chloe were quite naughty all day, refusing to help or stop fighting with each other.

Both wet themselves several times and Jenny soiled her panties. It was such a relief to settle the children at bedtime and even more of a relief when they all appeared to go to sleep.

However, this respite was short lived and it was in the early hours of the morning that Chloe screamed out.

This in itself was unusual as she had not had the night terrors before. I went in to her and tried to settle her but she was having none of it so I took her downstairs in case Jenny woke up.

I asked Chloe if she had had a bad dream and she said she had.

I had been thinking for some time now about how I could make these children feel safer and how I could get them to talk about their experiences and actually 'dump' them.

I had either heard or read an article about getting rid of bad experiences by literally writing them down and throwing them in the bin. I thought, well, you've got nothing to lose so why not try it with these children and there's no time like the present.

I asked Chloe if she would like to throw the dream away and she gave me a puzzled look. I gave her a hug and said "If you let me write down what you say, we can then put it in a bag, screw the top up and throw it in the bin." While I was talking, Chloe was laying on the settee, groaning and touching herself between the legs, sobbing, relaxing and stiffening alternately.

When she said yes, I got a carrier bag for her to throw the dream into and a pen and piece of paper. We then had the following conversation;

Me: Who was in your dream?
Chloe: Grandad
Me: Where were you?
Chloe: In my big bed, granddad was with me.
Me: What did he have on?
Chloe: No clothes. He took his pants off.
Me: What, Granddad had no pants on?"
Chloe: He showed me his willy.
Me: Where was it?
Chloe: On his self.

Chloe pointed between her legs.

Me: Was it a big or a little willy?
Chloe: A big one.
Me: What did you do?
Chloe: He said hold it.

At this I held up a finger and asked her to show me how. Chloe said it wasn't big enough so I held up two fingers. Still she said it wasn't big enough. When I held my hands together she used both her tiny hands and imitated masturbation.

Me: What happened then?
Chloe: It went little.
Me: Was it dry?

Chloe: No, it was wet and all over my legs. Granddad went wee all over my legs.
Me: Did anything else happen?
Chloe: Granddad tickled me.
Me: Where did you get tickled?
Chloe: On my self.
Me: Was it nice or did it hurt?
Chloe: It was nice.
Me: Did it ever hurt?
Chloe: Only my bottom.
Me: Have you any more bad dreams?
Chloe: No. I want to go to bed.

To be honest I was quite relieved that this conversation had come to an end.

I had not been prepared, despite knowing that she had probably been sexually abused, to hear such a little mite disclose her grandfather doing these things with her.

It was bad enough knowing that parents abused their children, but, somehow, grandparents seemed so wrong. I don't mean more wrong, just that my maternal grandparents were still alive and I couldn't even begin to imagine their horror if they knew about this.

Nor for that matter, what my parents would think if they knew, as they had always been so protective of me and my siblings as we had grown up and to a degree, still were (and are to this day).

After throwing the carrier bag and its contents in the bin I tucked Chloe back into her bed, before retrieving the bag from the bin, tucking its contents away so I could give them to Julia.

I spent a restless few hours before the children woke mulling over what I had been told.

Thank goodness this wasn't going to be my problem for the next two weeks I thought, rather selfishly, as I lay there in the dark.

Chapter 18

As a family we had a brilliantly relaxing two weeks, lazing around and having long walks over the moors during the day and evenings around the bonfire where we cooked our meals and sang camp songs.

We stayed in what our children lovingly called 'the baby house' but had once been a cow shed and had been converted into a cabin by my Uncle.

It was tucked away and even knowing exactly where it was, it could easily be passed. One year we had our extended family coming to visit us and even with the children shouting in the 'garden' and the camp fire billowing up smoke they couldn't find us as it the place was so secluded.

All too quickly our holiday was over and it was time to head home.

We'd hardly unpacked the car when Anna phoned to say she'd kept a diary of events for me to pass on to the social worker and to confirm we would be collecting the girls the following day.

We chatted for some time while she briefly outlined events of the past two weeks, saying she had done what I advised her should either of the girls have bad dreams, telling me that Chloe had had two bad nights while we were away.

Both had been on a Sunday.

Their Sunday routine had been the same as when they were home with us, the usual amount of time being spent at church in the morning and relaxing in the afternoon either at home or down the park. The only difference was that when we went to church we were with the children and tended to sit at the back, while Anna and her family sat in the front row of seats.

The girls, Anna told me, had settled very nicely for three days, with the exception of emptying a bottle of shampoo into the bath one evening and a few squabbles, when Chloe had had her first night terrors.

Anna said she had tried several times to resettle Chloe but had to resort to bringing her downstairs. Chloe kept talking about monsters hurting her and was quite agitated.

Once she was downstairs Anna asked if she'd had a bad dream. When Chloe said she had Anna had asked if she wanted her to throw it away "like Lizzie does" and went to get a bag.

The following conversation then took place;

Anna: How do the monsters hurt you?
Chloe: They bleed on me.
Anna: How?

Chloe: They scratch me.
Anna: Where?

At this point she pointed to different parts of her body. She was very agitated all the time. She then wanted her dolly and said the monsters would get her. Anna asked her who they were.
Chloe: monsters.
Anna: What else did they do?
Chloe: Put their willy on me.
Anna: Where?

Chloe pointed to her 'self'.

Anna: Anything else?
Chloe: Yes, they peed on me.
Anna: Did they do anything else?
Chloe: Yes, they made the cat bleed.
Anna: The cat?
Chloe: Yes, the pussy cat.
Anna: Who are they?
Chloe: Monsters.
Anna: What did they do when they made the cat bleed?
Chloe: They drank it.
Anna: Was the cat dead?
Chloe: No it was wobble bleed.

(When I read this I thought, knowing Chloe, she meant the cat was still alive but not walking).

Chloe kept saying there was another little girl there who was calling out for her sister, Jenny.

Anna had asked Chloe where she was when all this happened and she said in a room with flowers on the wall. The monsters were there, so was her sister and this other little girl.

Chloe seemed to settle once they had thrown this dream in the bin and seemed okay over the following week.

Anna told me that the following Sunday they'd had a similar experience with Chloe.

They'd had a good day out, going fishing and taking a picnic for lunch. When they got home Jenny settled quickly to sleep but Chloe was very unsettled.

Again she came down for a chat after having night terrors, saying that her 'self' hurt. Anna had asked if she had bumped herself and she said "No, the monster did it".

Anna: Did what?
Chloe: Scratch me.
Anna: Where?
Chloe: All over.

Anna had then asked Chloe to point where she had been scratched and she pointed all over her body.

Anna: Did the monster do anything else?
Chloe: Yes.
Anna: What?
Chloe: Put his willy on me.
Anna: Did you have any clothes on?
Chloe: No.
Anna: Did the monster?
Chloe: No.
Anna: Where did he put his willy?

Chloe had pointed to various parts of her body again, saying *"on my boobies and my head and my face and mouth. It's not nice is it?"* she had asked.

Anna: No it's not, did he do anything else?
Chloe: Yes, I had to stroke his willy first while I was lying down then I had to stand up then lay down again.
Anna: What happened then?
Chloe: He put his willy on my 'self', in out, in out, in out.
Anna: Did it hurt?
Chloe: Yes and I cried and he laughed at me.
Anna: Did he stop when you cried?
Chloe: No. He kept on, in out, in out.
Anna: What happened then?
Chloe: He wee'd on me.
Anna: What did he do then?
Chloe: He got my sister Jenny.
Anna: What did he do to her?
Chloe: The same as to me.

Anna said that at this point Chloe was very upset so she got a bag, threw the monster in and put him in the bin.

Chloe then had a restless night, crying out in her sleep periodically until the morning.

With the exception of the two night terrors for Chloe the holiday had almost passed without incident.

The girls had spent some time arguing with each other and refusing to do as they were asked, Jenny had wet herself almost daily and Chloe had done the same on some days.

Most nights Chloe had been concerned that the monsters may come and get her but had settled, most days Jenny was emotional but unable to explain why.

The day before they were to return to our home Anna found Jenny with her hand in Chloe's knickers.

Jenny, Anna said, had started to cry as soon as she was seen and had said she wouldn't do it again because "it's not nice."

So, after a wonderfully relaxing fortnight we were home.

Tonight I was going to sleep soundly in my own bed in a contented home with three happy children.

Tomorrow Jenny and Chloe would be home and we would start work again.

Chapter 19

Jenny and Chloe arrived home and seemed to be fine. They played nicely for a while, then argued then fought, because Jenny wanted to cuddle Chloe and Chloe wanted to play.

It wasn't until two days later that Chloe started talking about monsters to me.

Her first and only comment on this day was that they were not nice and wear masks, said as she circled her face with her little hand.

The following day however, things got a little concerning. The children had all started back at school after the summer holidays and Chloe had a doctor's appointment.

As we walked along I bought up the bad dreams she'd been having in the hope that she may make a disclosure to the doctor who could then be able to direct us to a more specialised form of support for the children and us:

Me: You know you can tell doctors about bad dreams.

Chloe: Yes, all the monsters.
Me: Do you like the monsters?
Chloe: No, they are all horrible.

Because of the girls' preoccupation with monsters and the incident with our poor dog, along with my concerns about what Anna had recorded while we were on holiday, a concern was forming in my mind.

I believed in God, therefore, I believed in the Devil. Chloe had started her 'big' disclosures after going to church without her 'comfort zone' of me, Howard and our family.

She had been sitting in unfamiliar seats and up close to our minister. This I figured may have been the trigger so I took a chance and asked Chloe "Do you know who you serve?"

Chloe: Yes.
Me: What, like I serve God, who do you serve?
Chloe: The monsters and I hate them. They put their willy up my 'self' and wee'd. They're mucky pups...mucky pups.

The rest of the day passed without incident.

Chloe had said nothing to the doctor about her bad dreams, though he made a referral for her to see a specialist because in his opinion there were signs she had been sexually abused.

When all the children were home they played together for a while, then Jenny and Chloe started looking through a Christmas catalogue that was on the table. I asked them why we celebrate Christmas and they laughed at me saying they didn't know. I told them it was someone very special's birthday so Jenny said, "Claire's! James's! Edward's"!

I then told them it was Jesus birthday. I then asked them if they knew what Halloween was and Chloe shouted *"Willies! It's when the willies come!"*

This was concerning.

This was very concerning. What the hell had happened to these children?

The following day, Sunday, Chloe had another bad dream that she wanted to throw away before going to bed.

Chloe: It's the monsters.
Me: What monsters?
Chloe: Granddad. He puts a mask on like a monkey. It's a monster.
Me: Who is with you?
Chloe: Me and Jenny and Louise.
Me: Has Louise got long hair?
Chloe: No, short like me and brown like me but curly.
Me: What happened?
Chloe: They put blood on me. All on my belly and wee'd on me.
Me: Where did they get the blood?
Chloe: A chicken. They put it in a hole but it got out 'cos it didn't like it.
Me: Who was there?
Chloe: Granddad. I don't like him. He's a monster with big arms.
Me: Is there anything in the room or are you outside?
Chloe: Seven.
Me: Seven?

Chloe: It's a number. I didn't have my clothes on. They put blood on my belly and wee'd on me.

By now I was getting quite concerned as this sounded scary and more ritualistic by the moment and I didn't know much about these sorts of set ups. I had been brought up in the church so had a strong faith in my God.

I prayed like never before that He would keep my children safe from whatever was haunting these two small scraps of humanity.

Me: You look tired, do you want to put more in the bag or go to bed?

I was so hoping she would want to go to bed and not tell me anymore.

I never wanted either of them to tell me anymore, but knew that soon, Jenny would start to talk about her life.

I felt sure that Jenny was biding her time, waiting to see my reaction to Chloe, before she told me more shocking details.

When Jenny finally spoke, which was, unknown to me, only weeks away, I felt the bile rise, the tears were forced back and the fear levels were raised.

I wanted to cry for these children. Scream out for them to be kept safe. And all I could do was sit, stay calm, carry on feeding the baby and, much as I didn't want to know or hear what they were saying; kept them talking.

Five days later both Jenny and Chloe were being naughty and generally disruptive. When we were on our own I asked them why they were playing up, not that many three and five year olds know the reason for most of what they do, they just do things because they want to without thought of consequences.

But we sat, the three of us, at the table and talked about the day and what had been going on for each of us. Chloe started talking about a bad dream. Jenny was sitting with us and getting very agitated.

Me: You have bad dreams too don't you Jenny?
Jenny: Yes.
Chloe: It's monsters.
Jenny: Big one's with....
Me: With what?
Chloe: It's monsters with willies that wee on you.
Jenny: It's granddad.
Me: Is anyone else with you?
Chloe: Yes, a girl.
Me: What's her name?

At this point Jenny became very agitated and got down from the table.

Chloe: Louise.
Me: Oh, Helen (I said this just for a reaction and clarification that Chloe would repeat her last comment).
Chloe: No! I said Louise.

Jenny now started laughing and trying to change the subject.

Chloe wanted to carry on talking, and did so. Jenny now looked a Chloe and I felt a warning was given that enough had been said.

The conversation ended with the girls chatting about the number seven. It's on a wall or floor or all over the place. No other number would do though.

It had to be the number seven. Why?

A couple of days later both girls became upset when they went to bed. They were both complaining that they were afraid of the 'smell'.

I couldn't smell anything and asked what they were talking about. They then said that they'd liked the rides, but not the house with the smell and the monsters. It frightened them.

Both of them were crying and it took me some moments to realise they were talking about the haunted house that we had gone in to when we had spent the day at a theme park some two months earlier.

At the time they had appeared to have enjoyed themselves and when I checked back through my diary, I read that they had behaved themselves well all day, even the travelling hadn't been a problem, though we had gone by coach rather than car, and that they had then settled well that night.

It just goes to show how deep these children buried things and how time passes without a word being said until something triggers off a memory.

Chapter 20

Going to church was also now becoming problematic, as Jenny and Chloe became convinced that the monsters were there as well.

Chloe refused to go in the crèche with the other little ones, needing the constant reassurance that me or Howard were close to her and that Jenny was within eyesight as well.

Jenny and Chloe had also started to lash out at the dog. For his part, the dog mostly avoided them by either staying out of the room or hiding under the settee.

One day Jenny went to drag the dog from his hiding place and he snapped at her. Our poor little dog, who had always been so gentle even if a bit scatty, had actually snapped and I think had I not shouted at him, he may well have bitten her.

That evening, once Jenny and Chloe were in bed, Howard and I sat with our children.

We had to ask them a very important question and ask for an answer, without letting them know the details of why the girls were behaving as they were.

Edward, James and Claire sat listening to me as I said "We have a problem. Today the dog snapped at Jenny. I thought he may bite her. We have to make a very hard decision and that is, do we keep the dog, or do we foster?"

Their little faces just looked at us and they asked if Jenny had hurt their pet.

I then explained that Jenny and Chloe had not been looked after properly and they were afraid of dogs because one had probably hurt them in the past.

Howard told them that we would both understand if they wanted us to stop fostering as we knew how special their dog was, especially as it was a present from their big brother who they all adored.

In all honesty; at that moment I think I almost wanted our children to say they wanted to keep the dog and send the girls away.

Claire, our youngest at just seven years old, spoke first.

She just looked at me and her dad and said "But this is their home mummy. We can't just make them go."

The boys agreed, saying that their 'sisters' were more important.

For Howard and I this was an enormously emotional moment.

We had made the decision to foster. We had discussed as best we could with our young family about having brothers and sisters coming to live with us that were in no way related to us. We had explained that their toys may get broken and they would have to share everything...especially their time with us, but we had never expected to have to say they would have to choose between the children and a special pet, something living and breathing that they loved so much.

We hadn't been able to explain the intricacies of fostering as they were so young and, in all honesty, we didn't know them ourselves when we had first started fostering.

In that short space of time Howard and I knew we couldn't have asked for more from our children, than that they accept, unquestioningly, all that they had to live with.

Our children knew they were safe and loved so very much.

They also knew, without having any detail that Jenny and Chloe needed to be with us, needed to be cared for and loved by our family, as they were.

The next day I managed to get the dog on a 'dog adoption' scheme as I had promised the children we wouldn't have him put down.

The week between making the decision to have the dog on this scheme and him actually going was quite an emotional one for everyone. I'm sure our children were, to some degree quite angry and upset at the choice they'd had to make, but they didn't show it to Jenny and Chloe.

The day the dog went there were tears at bedtime from everyone. Howard and I had our own guilt to cope with because of the choice we had given to our children, but we knew it had to be theirs to make.

It would be many years before we would risk getting another dog.

Chapter 21

Because Chloe was only at playschool three half days a week it meant that I had quite a bit of time every day on my own with her. Chloe could be very funny one minute and an emotional wreck the next.

Most of her talking though was done in the evening or overnight. Day times were for playing and cuddles with the odd bit of information coming out, almost as if she was sounding me out for bigger revelations that evening or night. I sometimes thought that perhaps Jenny was telling Chloe what little bits to disclose, using her as a sounding board, preparing me for more disturbing information that was to come.

One day, Chloe had spent most of the morning playing nicely with the baby dolls, nursing them, feeding them and giving lots of cuddles. After lunch we sat and spent time drawing pictures and colouring in.

Chloe, although occupied with this task was becoming quite agitated. She kept talking about lions and monsters. She said "lions kill people". I asked her if she had ever seen a lion kill someone and she said she had; a baby.

That evening Chloe lay on the floor and sobbed and writhed around. She wouldn't stop even when I tried to soothe her, but asked for a bag.

As the other children and prospective adoptive parents for our baby were around we went up to my bedroom to talk.

Chloe: I don't like monsters because they hurt you. They cut me and made me bleed here and here (indicating arms and legs). They're not nice.

As Chloe had spoken earlier about numbers I asked who number one was and she said it was her. When I asked who number two was she gave the same answer, saying she was a monster.

I reassured her she was a lovely little girl but she insisted; young as she was; that she was bad and a monster. She then asked for some cream to put on her leg where she had a small cut after falling over earlier in the day.

Then she ran downstairs with the bag, telling everyone that she had spat the monster out and that they were in the bag to be thrown away. Fortunately this went over the heads of our children and the prospective adoptive parents were so besotted with their baby that they didn't seem to notice.

Later that night Chloe woke crying and came downstairs:

Me: Do you want to talk?
Chloe: Yes.

Me: What about?
Chloe: Monsters. Glynn.

I recalled my friend, also a foster carer, had a little boy some time back that Chloe had insisted on calling Glynn, though this wasn't his name. This is why I had asked again this evening who Glynn was.

The last time I had asked Jenny had been around, Chloe had become agitated and refused to say but Jenny had just looked at me and said, all matter of fact "Oh, he's just a man who chases after you and kills you with a knife".

Me: Will you tell me who Glynn is?
Chloe: Yes. He's good.
Me: What does he do?
Chloe: He cut.
Me: What with?
Chloe: A knife.
Me: A big or little knife?
Chloe: A big one.
Me: And then what does he do?
Chloe: And then he just smacks people.
Me: Does he do anything else?
Chloe: Yes.
Me: What does he do?
Chloe: He's naughty. He smacks and touches me on my 'self'.
Me: Do you have clothes on?
Chloe: Yes.
Me: Anything else?
Chloe: Yes. Smacking.
Me: Who else is there?
Chloe: The monsters.

Me: What are they called?
Chloe: Monsters.
Me: How many?
Chloe: one, two, three, four, five.
Me: Who's number one. What's their name?
Chloe: Seven.
Me: Seven? Who's number seven?
Chloe: Seven.
Me: Yes, seven. But what is sevens name?
Chloe: Louise.
Me: Is Louise a lady or a little girl?
Chloe: A little girl.
Me: What does Louise do?
Chloe: Scribble.....nice....not allowed....she's not allowed felt pens, only me aren't I? She does spanking.
Me: She spanks people or they spank her?
Chloe: They do it to her.
Me: Does she like it?
Chloe: She cries and she smacks me.
Me: That's not nice is it?
Chloe: No.
Me: Who else is there? Who is number two?
Chloe: Grandad was a monster.
Me: What number monster was granddad?
Chloe: Green and yellow.
Me: Did he have a number?
Chloe: Yes.
Me: What number?
Chloe: Me.
Me: What number were you?
Chloe: Seven. Seven, aren't I mum? (Chloe and Jenny had called us mum and dad almost from day one).
Me: I don't know sweetheart, I wasn't there was I.
Chloe: No.

Me: What did number seven do?
Chloe: Monsters.
Me: Yes. What did the monsters do to you?
Chloe: Bark at me. Paint on my belly.
Me: Anything else?
Chloe: Yes.
Me: What?
Chloe: Did painting. Shoes. Paint me.
Me: Did you like the monsters?
Chloe: No. The monsters won't go away.
Me: Where are they now?
Chloe: In my belly. Can you draw a belly?
Me: In a minute we'll draw a belly. Did you have your clothes on?
Chloe: They take my clothes off and then walk about me. Can you draw a mouth mum?
Me: Yes.
Chloe: You haven't drawn a mouth have you mum.
Me: One minute… There. A mouth. Happy?
Chloe: Yes. They do poo on me. Can you draw a 'self'?
Me: I don't know what it looks like. Would you draw one?
Chloe: After a drink.

We had a drink.

Chloe: Can I do colouring?
Me: Yes, but shall we write down what the monsters did to hurt you first?
Chloe: Yes.
Me: What did they do?
Chloe: They smack us.
Me: And?
Chloe: Smack us and just smack our 'self'. Just smacking.
Me: Did the monster have clothes on?

Chloe: No clothes on and they look at me and no clothes on and I want clothes back on. But they keep my clothes off and their clothes off. They have willies and 'selfs'.

Me: So they are men and ladies?

Chloe: Yes.

Me: How many of them?

Chloe: They are people.

Me: How many people?

Chloe: But I don't like the monsters. Can you not go there to the monsters house? This is not the monsters house is it?

Me: No. Whose house is the monsters house?

Chloe: One, two, three, four, five people and me, but I don't like to go there 'cos I didn't like the smell I didn't. Granddad lived there but I didn't like him to live there 'cos he's my granddad isn't he mum?

At this point Chloe stopped talking or listening to me so I gave her a big hug, reassured her that she was a very good girl for throwing all these bad dreams and monsters away and tried to settle her to sleep.

Within the hour she was back up crying and saying there were still monsters around.

Me: Who are they?

Chloe: Numbers.

Me: Who's number one?

Chloe: Louise.

Me: Is Louise a little girl or a lady?

Chloe: A lady.

Me: Who is number two?

Chloe: Granddad. They hurt me and wee on me. It's a big willy and granddad is jumping up and down on the bed. He asked me to hold his willy and move up and down like this (she demonstrated on my arm) and then wee'd all over me. I don't like the monsters. It's all mucky. They have willies and 'selfs' and go up and down on mine and Louise's beds and don't have clothes on.

Chloe finally settled to a restless sleep just before midnight. I did the same, though mulled over recent events.

These two little girls had definitely been somewhere and seen something that no little ones should go or see.

From what Chloe was saying it appeared that she had not only been sexually abused, but also involved in some sort of satanic/ritualistic abuse.

Men *and* women were apparently involved in hurting these children. I wondered how many more children might have been involved.

I remembered Julia saying that their mother seemed to 'sacrifice' her children to her father, then, after a short time, guilt appeared to settle in and she would take them back, only to return them when he threatened to disown her.

The chances were that she too had been a victim of this sick bastard.

Chapter 22

The following week went past with Chloe being very emotional, but not having the words to say how she felt, or being just too scared to say them.

Nights were awful and full of the night terrors, with one or both of the girls waking up screaming and crying. Both girls would be playing okay then suddenly become totally vacant and stare off into space or become extreme in their aggression towards each other, fortunately they tended to keep their aggression at this time just for each other.

Our children tended to keep out of their way as they didn't know what to expect at any given time.

Chloe played with her dolls most days, doing all the nice things that kids do with dolls. She copied me lots of the time so if I was sat feeding the baby, she sat beside me.

Sometimes though, she would hide her baby under the blankets on the floor because the monsters were going to get it. When she did this we would go through the now normal conversation of the monsters weeing on her baby and putting blood on it before she would pick it up and give it a big hug.

Since the start of the Summer school term Jenny had been very good at school.

Now she was soiling and wetting at home.

This pattern was to be followed for the duration of the girls' placement with us. Clean at home for one term then clean at school for the next, but *never* clean at both.

At the end of each term, depending on who had been getting the soiling, the teacher and I would smile and wish each other a good 'new term', knowing one of us was not going to enjoy it at all.

Towards the end of September, the girls started to become quite destructive with their toys.

One Saturday they beheaded a teddy bear both blaming each other.

The next day they pulled the ears off a cuddly rabbit and wrecked the playroom, once again pulling everything out of boxes, cupboards and drawers.

They woke screaming or singing at the top of their voices in the early hours of the morning and talk of monsters was almost non-stop.

When Howard drilled some holes in the wall Jenny was convinced a man would come out of the hole and a dead man be put back in it.

Finally though, we had a break through with social services.

They had managed to arrange for the girls to have some therapy. I thought my nightmare would finally be over now they would be getting proper professional help.

Oh how wrong I was.

The nightmare was in fact just about to start.

Chapter 23

When the therapeutic sessions started it was a new experience for me.

I had expected, in my naivety, that the girls would be given time to go through their terrors and have a proper 'dumping' session. What I hadn't realised was that the reality was they had an hour a week to 'dump' as much as possible.

This can't be done quickly though, as they needed to get to know and trust the person doing the therapy.

I was not allowed to participate in these sessions as they may want to say something that they don't want me to hear, therefore, I can't give any advice to the therapist as to when the girls are ready to talk by the way they are playing with the toys or by their body language.

Without knowing the person you are giving therapy to you have to learn their signs of when they are ready.

No direct questions are to be asked.

By all accounts Jenny and Chloe said nothing of any concern while with their new therapist.

However; as we left the first session both girls were ready to talk but were high as kites and just ran around when we got home screeching and waving their arms in the air like demented sparrows.

The good side to this was that they tired themselves out and slept fitfully for the first time in weeks even though they had said nothing.

Over the following two weeks the girls were very excitable, extremely irritable, argumentative and aggressive towards everyone. They had huge reserves of energy and would run the two miles to school in the mornings and trudge home at the end of the day.

Chloe was good at playschool and mostly played nicely when we were alone together.

Some nights we would find Chloe asleep on the bathroom floor and even though she didn't wake when we put her back in her bed she would kick or hit out as we did so.

They both needed constant reassurance that there were no monsters in our home and that they couldn't get in.

To be honest, I was getting a bit concerned about the bloody monsters myself as I reckoned God is everywhere, therefore the damned devil must have his access points as well.

He certainly did with these two children.

I checked my bible most days to make sure the page hadn't been turned. Paranoia I know, but my little rituals helped me sleep better when I had the opportunity.

Chapter 24

The scream; when it came was unlike anything I had ever heard before.

It was so piercing it made every hair on my body stand on end, and the feeling of terror I felt then, in that instant has never gone away.

I flew out of my bed and ran into the girl's room, convinced that something truly, utterly devastating was happening to one of the children.

Jenny was sat in her bed, staring quite vacantly at the wall. She had soiled herself and seemed totally bewildered.

My heart was racing and I actually had to look around for the cause of this little lady's distress.

If I, as an adult, felt real physical fear at that moment, in that room, what the hell did this child feel? I had to try to calm myself down while at the same time trying to comfort Jenny.

Mustn't let Jenny see me shaking. Mustn't let her see tears of fear were escaping from my eyes.

Fear of what, I didn't know. But it was a very real fear. I had to reassure Jenny that all was well and she was safe.

But how do you do that when you don't feel safe yourself?

I spoke gently to Jenny, hoping the words were reassuring. Though Jenny was physically there and almost robotically allowed me to change her out of her soiled clothes and put fresh nightwear on her, the fear in her eyes showed she was miles away, somewhere my words couldn't reach.

Jenny allowed herself to be placed on the floor while I changed all of her bedding.

Her body, which had been rigid and shaking, slowly relaxed and she settled okay after a while. I remained shaken for the rest of the night.

Both bedroom doors remained opened.

After tea that day Jenny and Chloe had had a bath. While in the bath they started talking about granddad. I was sat in the bathroom at this time giving the baby his evening bottle.

Jenny: Granddad's got a big fat willy.

Chloe stood up in the bath and used a flannel to show how big, holding one corner between her legs and pulling the other towards the ceiling.

Me: What does granddad do with his willy?
Jenny: He lets us stroke it.
Chloe: They wee'd on us like this.

Chloe stood up with an empty bubble bath bottle held between her legs upside down so the water emptied out. Jenny did the same but used two empty bottles because "that's how big they were".

Jenny: Uncle Paul let us touch his willy but the hairs hurt.
Me: What hairs? Where were they?
Jenny: The hair on his willy. He put it down there and it hurt. Uncle Paul's only got a little willy, not like granddads. I sat in granddad's room in bed and touched his willy. Nana was beside him under the cover and she didn't know.

They then talked about monsters and said that granddad had a lion mask.

"The monsters killed our baby" they both said at once.
Me: Whose baby was it? Where did it live?
Jenny and Chloe: It was our baby. It lived with us. It was in the middle and we wanted to cuddle it. It was smaller than your baby. They cut it in the guts then wee'd all on it. Mummy Susan was there and she cuddled us. They let her touch their willies.

My stomach was churning. I could feel myself trying not to be sick at the detail these kids were giving me.

Had they actually seen a baby being killed? Had they been innocent witnesses to some sort of ritualistic murder of a tiny baby?

I held the baby I was feeding close and fought the tears of fear back.

I knew I had to just stay calm until they were in bed. Talk normal to them or they may clam up and say no more about what their lives had been before they came here.

I didn't want to know any more about their past than I did now, but knew that if I didn't listen to them calmly and pass on what was said, they would never get the help they needed and they needed that help now.

I needed that help now.

I was getting really scared for my family.

All the 'what if's' of 'them' knowing where we live crept into my mind at the most inopportune moments lately.

What if they stole my children because we had theirs?

What if they harmed my children?

What if they actually came and took Jenny and Chloe?

Talk. Talk to the girls and keep calm. I mustn't hold the baby too tight or he'll be crying as well.

I'm no bible basher but I reasoned that if God was in my home, the Devil may be as well and we just had to show *him* who was stronger.

Me: What did they do with the baby?
Jenny: I don't know. We were in a field. There were people but it was our baby and we was frightened.

Jenny then said that they had been in the house. They had cuddled their baby all day. It started to get dark and they went out of the back door and into a wood, carrying the baby. The baby was laid on a stone and cut open and all the insides were taken out and the blood was drank and smeared over every ones face and body. The insides (I believe she meant organs) were then put in a bowl and 'mashed' down, though she couldn't remember what then happened to them.

Both girls now became terribly worked up and excited. They screamed and laughed and cried. Both said that Uncle Paul's little willy was put up their 'selfs'.

There were faces with make-up. The faces were reds and greens with white mouths and brown eyes. Uncle Paul, granddad and mummy Susan had big dresses on. Paul and granddad had make-up on.

Both were concerned about going into the playroom after their baths because it was dark outside and the monsters could come in and get them. I closed the curtains against the darkening evening, reassuring Jenny and Chloe that they were safe and asked them to play nicely before it was time for their story.

Amazingly they settled okay at bedtime. Howard and I were the ones once again left sleepless and concerned for all of us.

Chapter 25

The following morning Jenny sat on the settee and wet her pants, soaking everything. She was very tearful and unsettled all day.

Chloe drew a picture of her worst dream and, as basic as it was it tied in with what she had said about being in the field with mummy Susan and the monsters.

The following day both girls were still emotional. They didn't want to settle to anything. Maybe it was they couldn't settle to anything.

I knew I had difficulty settling to anything and I was the adult. There were so many thoughts going through my mind, things I was trying to make sense of.

Jenny kept saying that mummy Susan had her baby and it was killed with a knife. They both kept thumping their dolls in the stomach saying "Kill babies, kill babies".

I kept our baby in sight all the time and couldn't leave him in the room even to pop out to the loo unless Howard was there to make sure he was safe as I was unsure if Jenny and Chloe, though they didn't have access to knives, would hurt him.

Following these disclosures the girls' behaviour became even more erratic.

They would constantly be touching each other's genitals.

One morning I went in to find Jenny on her knees with her nightie up around her ears with Chloe kneeling behind her, nightie around her waist doing a 'doggie', this being their words for their actions.

They both ignored me as they were engrossed in what they were doing with each other.

They would parade around their bedroom with no clothes on when they were supposed to be getting ready for bed, saying it was what granddad had shown them to do.

Jenny said that granddad liked them to walk around with no clothes on while he played with his willy.

Both continued to cry out in the night though seldom woke up. Both were very demanding and now, Chloe started to masturbate in front of me, though thankfully not in front of Howard or our children.

Finding ways to distract them from their strange behaviours was becoming an ever more inventive exercise. The playroom continued to get 'trashed' on a regular basis, though not regular enough for me to have a distraction plan ready and certainly not with any particular behaviours that would warn me as to when this would happen.

If only there was a routine to what they did, but there was none.

Chloe was now four years old and, when Jenny called her a baby one day she retorted that it was in fact Jenny who was a baby because she wore nappies to bed.

We had tried to get Jenny out of her nappy. Every time I told her she had been dry for a few days and asked if she wanted to stop wearing it she would be soaked that night.

It was her protection. She seemed to reason that no-one could get to her while she had that on.

Chapter 26

Come December and, with the disclosures some weeks behind us everything seemed to be settling down.

We had stopped going to church most weeks as it distressed the girls too much, but we took them to see the nativity play.

What a big mistake that was.

When someone said Jesus' name Chloe shouted out that he was a monster. That was a fun one to explain away over coffee after the service, though thankfully the children seemed relaxed and passed no more such comments.

The only person in the church who had any awareness of some of the issues within our home was our minister, after I had asked for advice when Jenny and Chloe had started talking about what appeared to be devil worship and ritualistic things I knew nothing about.

Trouble was; our minister had become extremely concerned for the safety of our children and advised

Howard and I to have Jenny and Chloe placed into another foster home. I don't think he understood that Howard and I couldn't do that.

How could we not only reject these very needy children; but also put another family through at best, what we were going through and at worse...something even scarier, knowing they wouldn't be given the whole story when the children moved in.

I could see the concern on his face every time we saw each other. Though the support I received from our minister wasn't the sort I'd wanted; reassurance that we would all be safe; what I got benefited our sons as they were taken out for snooker afternoons and given the opportunity to speak with someone who was not related to them or what was going on at home.

I don't know about now as our children are grown up, but therapy was seldom readily available for the children in the care system back then and certainly not available to children who were not in the system.

On Christmas Eve the local Round Table came round with a float decked out as a sleigh with Father Christmas on it.

They were waving to everyone and giving sweets to the children. Jenny and Chloe had been in the bath but I wrapped them in towels and took them into their bedroom so they could wave through the window while Howard went out to give a donation and receive some sweets for all of our children.

They were very excited and shouted "Hello Father Christmas" then Jenny waved and shouted "hello granddad".

Chloe then became upset and said she didn't like him getting into her bed because he wasn't nice.

Both girls then became upset and unsettled because they didn't want Father Christmas to come into their room while they were asleep.

It took some reassurance that he wouldn't enter their room but would leave all the presents downstairs.

Christmas day passed without incident and we appeared to settle down for a few days.

Chapter 27

As we celebrated the New Year we had a sudden death in the family and our lives turned upside down.

Obviously the girls picked up on the emotions we as adults were feeling.

Suddenly I couldn't spend all my days with Chloe as I had to be available for my extended family as well.

Both girls started acting up again.

Now they were going to the toilet together to watch each other as they did their business. The bickering and arguing increased and the talk about granddad and what he did was almost a daily topic.

The only saving grace was that our children seemed blissfully unaware of what the girls had been through, though this was mostly due to the fact that the girls did most of their talking at night while our three slept, or during the day when they were either out or playing.

The one thing our children couldn't miss though was the tantrums.

Jenny and Chloe would have major tantrums where they would suddenly throw everything they could get their hands on in the playroom all over the place.

They would rip books up, which our children found most upsetting as they are all book lovers; they also found the girls going to the bathroom together rather strange and would always alert me if they saw them enter the bathroom together so I could get the one not using the toilet out of the room.

Chapter 28

We had snow that year and the children all had fun in the garden making a snowman. Once he had been made and dressed we all stood back to admire their handy work. The snowman stood about four feet high and the children had given him a face using pebbles and a carrot and arms from the twigs in the garden. They had even wrapped a scarf around his neck.

Jenny got so excite she rushed over to him and with a huge smile clapped her hands gently on his cheeks...the look on her face as his head disintegrated was hilarious and we all laughed, including Jenny who helped make another head for the poor thing.

These moments of familial joy were few and far between so we made the most of those we had.

As my nephew was now at a local school he came home some evenings and Jenny had started playing with him and ignoring Chloe. In retaliation Chloe would hound them relentlessly and spoil any games they were playing.

One day Claire tried some new clothes on. Being a sensible little girl she had unwrapped them, tried them on and after showing me what she looked like put them in her wardrobe.

What she had forgotten to do was put the packaging in the bin.

Fortunately I had got into the habit of only allowing Jenny and Chloe a few minutes to get ready for bed before going up to help them, because this day they had gone into Claire's room and taken the plastic bag.

Jenny was pulling the bag over Chloe's head when I went into the room. I took the bag from her and asked her what she thought would happen to Chloe if I hadn't. Jenny's response was quite direct and totally cold. "Chloe would suffocate".

Chloe had gone through a phase of drawing all over Jenny's dolls, in retaliation Jenny took to scribbling all over the walls, one day scribbling from the hall all the way up the stairs to the bedroom, denying being the culprit when I came out of my room and saw her, pen in hand and nib on the wall.

The girls could now fight from dawn to dusk, but as soon as one of them was told off for anything, they would hug each other and defend each other totally.

Almost nightly they would be found in bed with each other. One night, after finding them touching each other again I asked them to stop, Jenny just kept saying "It's what my granddad taught me" over and over again. Jenny said her granddad liked to watch her play with Chloe.

A few days later Jenny asked me what I would do if her granddad knocked on the door. I asked her what she would want me to do and she replied that I should send him away because he's naughty.

She seemed quite obsessed about him finding her and needed a lot of reassurance that he couldn't because there were a lot of people looking after her, Howard and I being only two of the team.

Jenny was also, by now aware that the plan had been for her to have a new 'forever' mummy and daddy and was concerned that he may find their house and get her later. I reassured her yet again that he couldn't find her unless she went to see him and told him where she was.

She replied she'd never do that because he's bad and naughty and she doesn't like him.

Chapter 29

Due to the disclosures Jenny and Chloe had made not only at home, but also during their therapeutic sessions the plan was no longer for the girls to be adopted.

The department had held discussion with all external agencies and doctors involved in the children's welfare and had decided that a residential therapeutic unit would best suit their needs at the moment, as they appeared to be incapable of functioning in an ordinary family environment.

We had to agree with their findings as much as it was upsetting to think we could not prepare these little girls for a move to permanency via adoption. We had stopped talking about forever mummies and daddies some time ago, only telling the girls if they mentioned it that one day they would have their very own mum and dad.

The process of moving children on is long and drawn out whatever the plan is. We'd had meetings and panels but nothing had been finalised.

One day I'd had enough uncertainty and wrote to the director of social services, asking him if they would please put their duty to the children above the cost to the department.

I got a lovely letter back letting me know that everything they could do was being done and that they were in the process of identifying the right place for the girls to move to.

We could only wait now to be informed about where and when this was going to happen and keep on diarising what the children were saying and doing.

Chapter 30

Children in the care system have a statutory medical when they enter a placement and every year after that until they are placed for adoption or return to their birth family.

The day of Jenny and Chloe's medical arrived and off we went. The girls were well behaved while we were out and did all the bits they were asked to do, with the exception of Jenny, who did a little more than she was asked.

When the doctor went to listen to her chest she soiled herself! This was a quite deliberate act, and clearly showed she was distressed at that time. She was very quiet coming home and while she had her bath.

The next day Jenny was still clearly distressed and the girls played a game of giants and granddads. I asked who the giant was and they told me it was a big man who hurt little girls. When I asked if he hurt granddads I was told he didn't because he liked granddad.

They were playing with their dolls, acting as though the dolls were them while they were the giants. They hit the dolls and threw them around the room while squeaking "Help, help, the giants found us!" and "Now I'm going to get you. Take that and that" as they hit, kicked and threw the dolls around.

I had to stop the game and sit with Jenny and Chloe while I explained about how it's not nice to hurt little children and they ended up cuddling their dolls better, but didn't settle well at bedtime.

Over the next few days aggressive behaviour seemed to be the order of the day, culminating one morning as we were getting ready to go to school with a nasty assault on Claire by Jenny.

We were all in the hall. Claire asked Jenny to get her coat on and quick as a flash Jenny had her hands round Claire's throat and was squeezing tight.

Claire hit Jenny on her arm to make her let go, which she did and burst into tears saying she didn't know why she had done it.

Claire was visibly shaken and clearly upset by Jenny's actions. It seemed like every time we took a little step forward we soon had to take a big step back with the girl's behaviour.

We were still waiting to hear news about when the children would be moving to their new home and now it was becoming urgent, as we couldn't let our own children be put at risk of injury.

Now we found we also had to give Edward, James and Claire almost daily reassurance that they were safe and our lives would soon be changing, though having to do this without giving them the secret that

Jenny and Chloe would be leaving to live somewhere else sooner rather than later.

Our children had never experienced a child leaving us to go anywhere other than home or to a forever family and we knew at some time we would have to explain to them that sadly, even we could not do enough for Jenny and Chloe.

Chapter 31

Jenny's birthday came and went. We had a birthday party for her, inviting all the children in her class and she got lots of lovely presents. She was wonderfully behaved on the day but by the end of the week almost all of her new toys were destroyed and in the bin.

Jenny was also now, from what Chloe was saying, touching her intimately every day. Chloe would come down some nights crying that her 'self' was sore because Jenny wouldn't stop rubbing it.

Jenny would argue that Chloe asked her to touch her and that she did it because 'that's what granddad used to do,' and would always say she'd not do it again.

Unfortunately we didn't have the space to separate the children at night so it meant we had to pop up and down periodically throughout the evening checking that they were in their own beds. Chloe went back to shouting "Get your hands out my knickers" to let me know she needed us and gradually Jenny got the message.

Jenny and Chloe had been with us just over a year when Jenny screamed out in absolute terror one evening.

Howard was first up the stairs with me close behind him. Jenny was screaming for mummy and daddy but wasn't awake.

We managed to calm her down and she settled for a while, but was soon crying in her sleep again. This went on for about three hours with one or both of us running up and down the stairs.

After about two hours of Jenny crying, Chloe started as well, though neither of them actually woke up they were clearly both distressed and in the grip of some nightmare which neither of them remembered, or at least they appeared not to remember the next day.

One day shortly after the spring term started I was called down to the school. Jenny had set the fire alarm off and the whole school had to be evacuated.

She had been severely told off by the headmistress as the fire brigade had arrived and, though they knew it was Jenny who had set the alarm bells ringing, they still had to check the school was safe before allowing the children back into the building.

Jenny was very quiet as we walked home that afternoon and sat quietly as I explained to her how naughty her actions had been. I don't know if she grasp the enormity of what she had done because she hadn't been involved in a real fire and trying to get a seven year old to realise that every false alarm means someone may actually die in a real fire because there are no free fire engines to attend is difficult to do.

Also, because she had been through so much, I didn't want to scare her any more than I had to.

Around this time we also had a phantom in our home that loved toilet rolls. They would vanish overnight. We could go through eight or more rolls in a week and even as large a family as we were, none of us had that bad a digestive system that we needed to sit for hours!

This went on for a couple of weeks before Jenny and Chloe got a bit carried away and just shredded a whole roll and left a trail from the bathroom to their bedroom, in, around and under their beds.

They couldn't deny it in the morning when I went into their room as it looked like a snowstorm had struck in the middle of the night. I had never seen tissue torn into such tiny little pieces before and had to give them points for their commitment to a job well done.

Their bedroom curtains also came in for a bit of redesigning.

I had never let children play with scissors unsupervised and kept them in the kitchen which had a gate across. This gate was kept shut at all times, even when I went into the kitchen I tended to go over the top rather than keep opening and closing it.

None of the children had any reason to enter the kitchen as they had access to the garden from the lounge and the only time they were in there was if we were baking, which I had long since stopped.

It doesn't appear to matter how many safe guards you put in place, a determined child will get round them, which is what Jenny and Chloe did.

One day, as I opened the curtains I noticed a nice kind of neat square had been cut from the corner.

There was no point asking who had done it as they would both blame each other, this simply meant we now had to find a 'hiding' place for the scissors, as the girls could clearly unlock the cutlery drawer.

I don't know what they wanted that scrap of material for though as I never found it. Maybe they were just a bit peckish that night, though more probably it got flushed down the toilet like so many other items did.

I also discovered a nice big hole of material cut from the front of Jenny's good coat, but as that had been in the wardrobe I didn't know who had done it, so patched it as best I could because I wasn't going to reward such behaviour with new clothes.

The level of violence the girls could use towards each other could also escalate.

One morning they were both screaming blue murder and when I went to them they had taken plastic belts from their wardrobes and were whipping each other with them.

We were on a constant level of high alert, wondering what next they would use to hurt each other.

As I said earlier, our home was not big enough to separate the children at night so they had no choice but to share a room, overnight and early morning was the only time they were unsupervised.

Chapter 32

Life was generally exhausting again and our holiday last summer seemed a long, long way off.

Jenny and Chloe would also now target Claire every now and then.

We hit a patch where they would ruin anything they could that belonged to her, sometimes creeping down in the night to empty her school bag and scribble all over her books or just ripping her books up and putting them back in her bag.

Claire was the only one who had to check her bag daily to make sure everything was as she had left it. This became the norm for Claire for the rest of the time Jenny and Chloe shared our home and never once did Claire ask that we speak to Julia about moving the girls to another foster home.

I know we could have made sure everything that belonged to Claire was in her room each night, but had we done that the girls may then have crept into her room and hurt her. We couldn't take that chance.

I was scared at the thought of what these little one's were capable of and our children were still young, Edward coming up to twelve, with James close on his heals at ten and Claire was now eight.

We could hardly say to them that one of the girls may hurt you while you sleep and give them that burden.

The thought that our children may be too scared to go to their beds at night and sleep; knowing they were possibly no longer safe didn't bear thinking about. They had to know they were safe in their own home; even if we didn't know it.

It was bad enough that I hardly slept and the tiniest noise seemed to have me awake, so God only knows how the girls had managed to get down stairs on the nights they did to get the scissors and do damage to Claire's belongings.

Nonetheless, without knowing what the girls had been through, our children were getting a bit stressed at the antics they got up to and the unpredictability of their actions, so they started to spend more time with each other or their friends.

This seemed to please both the girls as it meant they had more of me to themselves, which in turn just meant I became more tired and stressed, though it is very hard to recognise sometimes just how stressed you are.

The up side was that now, not only was I getting plenty of exercise with running up and down the stairs all evening, I was also losing weight, which, though I wasn't big to start with meant I could eat almost anything I wanted and not gain an ounce.

No problem there then because I rarely felt hungry at meal times so tended mostly to graze throughout the day. However what I didn't realise at the time was that I was heading for a nice hospital stay and major surgery!

Chapter 33

As the summer approached we had news that a therapeutic unit had been identified that could cater for the children's needs.

We were told that it was an ordinary house, much like ours, but with specialist carers which meant that Jenny and Chloe would have 'therapy' twenty four hours a day if they were awake and not at school or doing school activities.

This sounded absolutely ideal and we eagerly awaited the day Howard and I could visit to see what we thought.

The unit was miles from where we live and so we set off early one morning with the girls' new social worker, finally arriving just after lunch time.

From the outside the house looked pretty ordinary, just a normal semi in a normal street, one that you would pass without a second glance.

Inside there were three bedrooms, the largest of which was to be for Jenny and Chloe. Downstairs there was an office and a bedroom for staff as well as kitchen lounge and dining room.

The garden was a decent size so the girls would have plenty of room for outdoor play.

The only thing troubling Howard and me was the 'staff' bit. What happened to the 'home and foster parents' that we had been told about?

During our time there we were told that the unit has a shift system with four people on duty at any one time. The children would have therapy once a week which they would be taken to.

This was not what we had been told Jenny and Chloe were getting by a long chalk. They could have received that while living with us and in fact, they had been getting therapy over the past few months on this weekly basis and we had been coping with the backlash of behaviours caused by this.

But, as disappointed as we were at the actuality of this placement for the girls, I was too tired and, though still unknown to me, too ill to even argue about it.

We would just prepare the children for a move to their new home once we were told it was definitely going to go ahead.

We knew this would have to be done with the greatest of delicacy as Jenny had suddenly started talking about having a new forever mummy and daddy again, this time though she was positive about the prospect of her new family and us being a forever aunty and uncle.

Now we would have to, not 'shatter the dream', but gently nudge it a bit further down the road, while reassuring them that one day they would have everything they wanted, just not yet.

The final decision was made a few weeks before the school broke up for the summer that Jenny and Chloe would move during the second week of the holidays, this way they would have time to settle in their new home and our children would have a few weeks holiday with just me and Howard.

Though we were still not convinced that this was the ideal place for the girls we set about preparing them for this move, explaining that they would be living in a new home for a little while so they could get the help they needed in coming to terms with what had happened to them.

We had to make sure that they didn't look at this move as 'punishment' for any naughty behaviour but as something good that would lead to them having the family of their own that would always love them for the children they were and the adults they would grow to be.

This is quite a difficult thing to explain to young children as they seem to see everything in black and white and all they wanted was a forever family or, failing that, to stay where they were. There was also the problem with geographical distances. When a child is moving on in a planned way, as this was, it would be normal to take them to visit their new home at least once prior to moving in permanently. This couldn't happen with this move, though this was also because we didn't want to cause Jenny and Chloe concern about the issue of it being run by staff.

As the girls didn't travel well it was also decided that their possessions would all be taken up before them and we would go by train a few days later.

This proved quite a feat as they had accumulated a huge amount of toys and clothes, which all had to be packed and loaded into their social worker's car, which wasn't that big! However, we managed to get most of their toys, indoor and outdoor, loaded and sent on their way. A van was booked for the following week to take up everything that was left behind.

We had a big goodbye party for the children where they invited all their school and playschool friends, so our home was busting at the seams as about forty children all played together or fought each other.

It was total bedlam, but worth it.

Of course we then had a lot more to pack as each child bought presents for both of them!

Chapter 34

Finally the day to travel to their new home arrived.

It was quite chaotic as we still had the baby so had to pack not only Jenny and Chloe's belongings and ours, but also all the paraphernalia that goes with such little ones when spending a night away from home.

At last we were ready to go, me, Howard, Jenny, Chloe, one baby, four suitcases, pram and pram bag.

My poor Howard had a huge job on his hands trying to carry two cases with me pushing the others loaded on the pram and both of us trying to control two quite excited children.

We were lucky my parents were looking after Edward, James and Claire. This also meant my dad was on hand to take us to the station, though it was a cramped ride and took two journeys, the first leaving Howard and the baby with all the baby bits and our case at the local station, before returning to take me and the girls, with all the bits we had packed for them in the boot and around us in the car.

The whole journey actually was quite a nightmare as we'd thought we only had to get a train from our local station to London and that once we got to London and on the second train we would be able to relax.

No such luck because though we could chill for a few hours, the children needed feeding and then we found out we would have to change trains as the weekend service didn't go direct to our destination.

I had never realised before how tedious train journeys could be as I'd only done relatively short trips by train before. How the miles dragged so slowly below us as we journeyed on. We kept Jenny and Chloe occupied with drawing books and story books or playing I-spy and just chatting, and they both slept for a short time, which was heaven.

After an exhausting day we arrived late in the afternoon. We were met at the station and loaded into two cars and set off for the house that was to be Jenny and Chloe's home for the next year, which is how long we had been told they would live here before being ready to move forward with a permanent family.

Once we had settled the children and gone over their bedtime routine, which the staff disagreed with as it included Jenny having her nappy put on, Howard and I were taken to the small hotel we were staying in, which was some miles away from the girls.

We figured this was quite clever as we didn't have Jenny and Chloe's new address and we had no car; therefore we were stuck at the hotel until the 'staff' at the unit were ready for us to return the next day.

Tired and hungry, we unpacked and asked what food was available, only to be told that they didn't serve evening meals but that there was a nice pub about a mile up the lane, so off we went with the baby to find some food.

I must say this was a lovely pub serving great food and the locals were very friendly and of course, everyone loves a baby and strangers in the camp, so we had quite a bit of company as we ate.

After eating we headed back to the hotel. We had already decided we would have a nice early night but as we entered the building the lady who ran it asked if we could help them out.

Her sister, who lived abroad had come for a visit and was staying at their parent's home, but was due to fly out the following day.

Howard and I were asked if we would mind babysitting for them as they had already put their young daughter to bed.

They figured that as we were foster parents we had to be safe and trustworthy and we must have looked okay even if a little tired around the eyes.

Well, we weren't doing anything else so we were shown into the lounge and told to help ourselves to whatever we wanted from the kitchen and off they went.

Within ten minutes we were playing with their little girl who had woken and come down looking for mummy and daddy, to be faced with two strangers who were friendly enough to give her a drink and get some toys out and play until she was ready to go back to bed.

Chapter 35

The following morning we were collected and taken back to the home to spend some time with Jenny and Chloe and say our goodbyes.

We were told that though the children had seemed to settle and Jenny had been dry over night, she had subsequently squatted on the bed and wet herself in the morning.

It was a pity I hadn't been listened to as I had told them that Jenny didn't need a nappy because she wets the bed; she needed it as her protection, to keep her safe from anyone creeping in during the night and touching her.

One member of the staff asked us what we wanted to take back with us. This puzzled me and I asked her what she meant as I hadn't left anything at the house last night that belonged to me.

She quickly pointed out that Jenny and Chloe had an awful lot of clothes, including a couple of beautiful party dresses each, surely I could find a use for some of them. Also, they had a lot of rather large toys; prams, bicycles, desks, blackboards etc, would I like to take them back as they were not used to children arriving with so much and had limited storage space.

I had to explain that there would be another van of Jenny and Chloe's belongings arriving the following week and no, I would not be holding on to anything that belonged to the girls as it belonged to them and not me. How could this staff member justify me keeping things that not only had we purchased for Jenny and Chloe, but so had their little playschool and school friends, as well as our extended family members.

Still, you live and learn and I was going to learn something way down the line that was so very wrong about this place and the way they 'listen' to the children that was absolutely heart breaking.

But for now we said our goodbyes and set off home to spend some time with our children and get some much needed redecorating done to the girl's room in preparation for our next placement.

Chapter 36

The following week I telephoned Jenny and Chloe as I had been asked to, not that we needed asking because we were aware that children should never feel they have just been 'dumped' when they leave our home.

Unfortunately, I was told by whoever answered the phone that Jenny and Chloe were playing in the garden and that they didn't know if I was allowed to speak with the girls, so would I phone back the next day.

I phoned the next day and a few days later but was told each time that the girls were playing in the garden or out so in the end I stopped calling.

Eight months later, we received a letter from the principle officer of the home Jenny and Chloe were in.

It was a very nice letter giving us information on how the children had settled into their new home and schools and in many ways was an apology from them for not letting the girls keep in touch.

Apparently the staff had thought we were just tired out from the demands the children had placed on us and thought we considered our 'job' was complete. It was too late now though to even consider getting back in touch as we knew that by then Jenny and Chloe would just 'know' that they were just not 'good enough' for us to stay in touch. They would just 'know' it was their fault we had just walked away.

How very, very sad that professional people could do this to children they are supposed to support and protect.

My experience of good foster parents is that their job is never complete.

For ourselves we always have an open front door for all the children and their families, birth (if the children return home) or adoptive, who share our lives for however long or short a time they stay and over the years have enjoyed the occasional visit and letters from children that have brought tears and laughter into our lives.

Sadly, at the time of receiving this letter I was in hospital and just too ill and too tired to respond and then time just passed by and before I knew it a couple of years had gone by and there seemed little point in responding to someone who had probably even forgotten we existed..

Chapter 37

I can't remember how many years had passed when I received an article through the post.

There was a small covering letter, which was unsigned, to let me know this article had been printed in a social worker magazine and whoever sent it to me knew I would be interested to know how Jenny and Chloe were getting on, but also knew, like them, that I would be angered and outraged at the content of the article.

Apparently because Jenny and Chloe had so many nightmares where they woke screaming in the night their bedroom had been soundproofed. This was considered an appropriate action to be carried out in order for the other residents and staff to have a good night's sleep.

Wow, so that's all we'd have had to have done.

Soundproof the room and the problem goes away.

So much for the saying that is often quoted by social workers 'listen to the child'.

It appears this is okay for foster carers, but residential workers do not like to have their nights disturbed.

I was appalled as was Howard.

Surely if a child wakes screaming they need comforting and reassurance that all is well and they are safe.

It is very inconvenient to have to get up nightly to soothe a child when all you want to do is get a good night's sleep, but that is part and parcel of the work we take on.

I still wonder at the thoughts that must have gone through Jenny and Chloe's young minds to be in such terror and have no-one go to them when they were used to having a soothing voice come into the room before caring arms wrapped around them.

I try not to dwell on it though as it doesn't bear thinking about.

Chapter 38

Many years later, early one morning as Howard was leaving for work the telephone rang.

Howard answered the phone as I entered the room thinking it was a call from my friend who was due round later that morning. I stood listening and watching him. I knew from his response when he spoke that it wasn't my friend.

I heard him say "No. That can't be our Jenny" and stood still.

Something must have happened to Jenny. We'd heard nothing for years apart from that she and Chloe had been placed with adoptive parents and were settled.

Howard paled and thanked the caller for letting us know.

After hanging up, he asked me if I had seen any articles in the papers about a little girl that had gone missing. Though we have the papers I don't really read them, especially articles about children being abused.

Even after all these years of working with the damage that adults do to children, I find it impossible to understand how anyone can find pleasure in harming someone, old or young, that is vulnerable. Therefore, perhaps shamefully, I tend to only scan these articles as opposed to read them.

I had skimmed over the articles of this missing child, had glanced at the picture and thought, she looks familiar, but I hadn't realised that it was Jenny.

Now she had been found dead.

Jenny had been found murdered.

Howard and I just looked at each other; there were no words we could use. It wasn't the local authority who phoned either; it was Jenny's headmistress from when she went to our local school.

How sad that even our own local authority didn't feel the need to prepare us for finding out about the death of one of 'our' children. Because that's what Jenny was, like all of the children that share our home for a short time, but claim a tiny piece of our heart for ever.

Even though we may never see them again once they move on to better things and that is what permanency is all about, better things.

Permanency is a better life without carrying the label of being 'in care'.

Poor, poor Jenny.

She'd had such a crap start to her little life and such a tragic end.

And poor, poor Chloe, who, having lost everyone from her past, was to lose so much more over the coming months.

Postscript

Some weeks after Jenny's death I telephoned the childrens guardian ad litem asking if I could send Chloe a sympathy card. This was agreed to and then I was asked if I could send her any photo's that we had of Jenny and Chloe taken during their time of sharing our family life. I explained that we had prepared a Life Story Books for both Jenny and Chloe prior to them leaving our home and they had taken them to the therapeutic unit when they left. These, rather unfortunately had been mislaid. As this was pre digital camera era we felt awful when we could only find a couple of pictures to send, as the originals and negatives had all been sent off with the girls. We live and learn! Afterwards I kept spares of all photographic evidence of family life, ready for anytime a child may ask for copies, having had the originals lost with the passing of time.

We sent a card to Chloe using her nickname, which I was told appeared to make Chloe happy. During this telephone call from the guardian I was given the shocking news that Chloe had moved from her prospective adoption placement as the parents could not cope with her behaviour after Jenny's death, and that she was now trying to settle into a new placement.

We have heard nothing from or about Chloe since that phone call many years ago.

We hope, wherever she is that she has managed to put the events of her childhood somewhere safe and has made a good life for herself, while we acknowledge that these memories will always be just a whisper away.

Justice, as there was some in this case, was for Jenny. Her murderer was caught, taken to trial and imprisoned. Poor Jenny, such a trusting child had been befriended by her murderer shortly before the brutal attack on her was carried out by this very sad adolescent, who had his own emotional problems.

Chloe sadly was denied the chance to say her goodbyes at Jenny's funeral as her birth mother claimed the body and held the funeral in the location that she lived.

The adults involved in the systematic abuse of both Jenny and Chloe, though known to the department of social services have, to my knowledge never been brought to justice or made to pay for the crimes they carried out against these two little girls, and who knows how many others.

It is very hard to bring perpetrators of child abuse to justice as quite often the child/children are of an age that they do not understand what is happening, or they are of an age when they can tell lies. Many children who have been abused learn to tell excellent lies as they desperately try to hide what is happening to them for fear of reprisals to them or their families, which makes bringing their tormentors to justice even harder.

LIZZIE SCOTT

Happily married for over 30 years and got four kids who somehow think they are adults...but I know I'm not old enough to be the parent of an adult, but I also know I was there at the births...says a lot about me does that :-)

All my adult life has been dedicated to the welfare of children and ensuring they get the best service possible from me and the professional groups that are supposed to represent them...I hope between all the adults we did a good job, but at the same time just know some kids got sold short by the system.

I adore my family. My husband, kids and grandchildren are the most important thing in life to me.

I love writing as well and have written some poetry that I have never been 'brave' enough to even think about having published...but my first novel...well, that's different because it's a story that needs to be told and I've known that for many years, it's just taken me a long time to get round to doing something about it. You see, I believe the criminal justice system in our country can be so very wrong...how can a group of grownups decide if a child has or has not been 'harmed enough' to warrant a payout?

And what do the courts make of multiple abuses?

Well, it appears sometimes that doesn't count...but it does to me. So I guess the biggest thing to know about me is that I care passionately about kids and the importance of a childhood...happily I'm still living mine even though I'm fortunate enough to be grandmother.

Mia

Ok...

I'm a foster carer who doesn't want this placement.

The department of Social Services know just how to apply pressure...

Oh yes...they get one very good, very friendly, very experienced social worker that I happen to have so much respect for, to make the call, knowing, just knowing that I will possibly surrender and agree to share our home with a child that, to be honest, was the last child in the world that I felt capable of caring for...

Felt capable of feeling for...

Felt capable of...of having anything to do with her.

Mmmm, sometimes I'm so bloody shallow you see.

I don't want people to look at me as I go about my business.

I don't want strangers giving me pitying looks or hurrying past pretending they haven't looked in my pram.

I don't want to give up any of the precious time I spend with my birth children and husband.

I want my life to stay just as it is.

Happy and contented.

Oh the lessons I was about to learn about happiness and contentment...